LEADERS SPEAK

How to Transform Your Career

And Life Through Public Speaking

Martha Sue
Like that
you own your
Game &
teach others
to do the same!
Jody Cross

Table of Contents

FOREWORD

Have you ever noticed a need in the marketplace and stepped up to fill it with a new business, process, or product? Over 25 years ago, I started BNI®, Business Network International, for this very reason — I recognized the need for a way to generate referral business and BNI was the solution I came up with. Because BNI continues to meet a need commonly felt by businesspeople across the globe, it has since become the world's largest business referral organization. Back in 1985, business owners and professionals had only two choices: networking groups that became too rigid with levels of fines and penalties, or the other extreme, groups that bordered on being social clubs, with little to no measurable results. There was a distinct need for a networking group that had both structure and accountability, where people could market their business or company in a results-driven, cost-effective way through the power of word-of-mouth marketing. BNI was started to meet this need and continues to offer professionals from a variety of industries the opportunity to increase their business, clients, and revenue through building and enhancing relationships; public speaking is at the heart of how this is done.

Public speaking engagements are a great approach to getting more business while you're working on your networking. When you schedule an appointment with someone you think might be interested in what you're selling, the time you spend with that one person is very important. So, imagine having that same time with 20 to 50 business people in your community all at once. This became a specific strategy for me in and of itself: to build my company through the word of mouth that comes from speaking engagements. This technique can work for almost any business. However, the key is to go in with information and education, not a huge sales pitch. Similar to networking, public speaking is ultimately about building relationships; yet some professionals don't spend enough time considering their audience before they speak. Or, they do learn about their audience but aren't sure how to incorporate what they learned into their speeches. Thus, the effect they can have on their listeners, and therefore on their own results, is limited.

With her Leaders Speak program, Jody Cross has developed an answer to the challenge of effectively connecting with an audience to successfully forge relationships and achieve optimum results. A few years ago, when Jody and I had our first meeting in person, we discussed the value that a mix of networking and speaking can provide. After sharing with me her philosophy and process on how to make presentations "all about the audience," I suggested that she write a book to share her strategy with the world. Now, she has done just that. She has created this invaluable resource, which you are now holding in your hand. Jody has developed a process that teaches business professionals how to connect with their audiences more deeply so their listeners will relate to, remember, and even repeat their message (ideally resulting in a referral to a new client who didn't even hear the speech). This makes it much more likely that the audience will be able to use the speaker's information and more probable that listeners will hire, buy from, or do business with that speaker. Not only does this mean a speaker can get more business immediately following a speaking engagement, it also means that by using Jody's method they can establish new relationships, which could bring them exponentially more clients and revenue over time. Instead of presenting the same speech every time you speak, it is this Leaders Speak process of making it about your audience which should be repeated every time.

Over the years, you have likely heard many different speakers presenting on numerous topics. Jody is spot-on when she says that the best speakers, by far, are those who truly connect with their audience by touching on what is important to those listeners. Public speaking has been a large part of my life, both as a business leader and an author. From my own experience, I can tell you without hesitation that this book is more than simply principal instruction on how to do public speaking — it also provides an entirely new mindset for many people. In addition to detailing an important philosophy, *Leaders Speak* offers readers a concrete program, which they can begin implementing immediately to improve their own speaking, consequently their audience's results, and ultimately their own results.

Jody consistently receives high praise from members of her own audiences and, through her Leaders Speak program, she is helping other business professionals around the world to obtain this same degree of success in their public speaking ventures. In addition to teaching people to improve as public speakers, she enables them to actually start enjoying their public speaking opportunities and have fun by becoming less nervous and more comfortable through making it "all about the audience." Jody saw a need in the business market and she has created her business, program, and this book to meet that need. She and her program have had a positive effect on the speaking skills, careers, and even the lives of many businesspeople thus far and I am honored to have been involved in this project. I commend you on the wise investment you are making by reading this book, and I wish you all the best as you venture forth in your business and speaking endeavors with the new skills and confidence I know you will gain from *Leaders Speak*.

Ivan R. Misner, Ph.D.
Founder of BNI®
New York Times Best Selling Author

INTRODUCTION

Have you ever found yourself so nervous before a speech that you wished you hadn't agreed to do it? Have you ever felt after a speech that it didn't go as well as you wanted even though you put a great deal of time into preparing for it? You are not alone. These types of reactions to public speaking are very common. The good news is you can change these views!

If you want to:

- Look forward to giving a speech
- Enjoy being at the front of the room
- Leave with the sense of accomplishment that you nailed it

then this book is for you.

Many people think that public speaking is an innate talent — either you're good at it or you're not. I beg to differ because I've seen countless people (with a wide range of presenting experience) change their careers and lives because they changed their public speaking.

Others believe that you just have to learn the tips and tricks of the trade in order to organize and deliver a speech the "right" way. However, this is actually dangerous thinking because then speakers put together one speech on one topic, figure that their work is done and give that same, canned speech to every audience they encounter, missing the mark with most of them.

Think about these two scenarios when YOU have been a listener:

1. Remember a time you were in an audience and you could tell that the presenter had recited this exact content before. Maybe you were insulted, maybe you thought it was still good information even though it didn't completely apply to you, or maybe you were even inspired at the time but found later that you were not really sure how to use it.

2. Now, think back to a speaker who actually spurred you to do something different after you left his or her presentation. If you can actually recall this event, then chances are that particular speaker used content, wording, and stories that related very directly to you.

This could have happened accidentally, if the presenter had experience or background similar to yours. It is so empowering to realize that speakers CAN do this consciously with each audience, even when it would appear that the speaker and listeners have little in common.

You just reminded yourself what it was like to be a member of an audience. This leads you in the right direction. To become a truly great speaker, you have to put yourself in the shoes of YOUR audience, to empathize with them. You need to do this specifically for each group of listeners on each occasion.

For many of us, this is changing the way we usually think. Instead of coming at a speech from solely our own "expert" view, we need to approach it from the perspective of our audience. What brought the listeners here today? What message could they walk away with that will make their lives better? When you ask these questions, you will quickly find that your thoughts about yourself, what you want to sell, even your own insecurities begin to melt away. You are left with a new way to connect with your audience that none of the listeners will ever forget. Do that, and you can change lives.

Nobody begins as an expert at anything!

For more than 20 years, I've been speaking in public and listening to others speak. For 17 of those years, as a college instructor and through my training business, I've been teaching others how to improve their own public speaking. I did not start out knowing everything I've included in this book. Over time, I noticed that when I adapted to my audience (group of listeners) the way that I would adapt to a friend (one listener), I got a better reaction. Well, what is the difference besides the number of listeners? The answer is I acquired knowledge and understanding of my audience. It is easier to be other-oriented when you're talking with one person you know very well. The challenge is how to do that on a larger scale with people with whom you have little or no history. An audience of many people is still made up of individuals who care about their own lives. I had to figure out how to get to know and understand those individuals in order to connect when speaking to them.

This task is easier and less time-consuming when you realize how to take what you do naturally with one friend or family member and apply that to a group. Although we've developed this skill to the point at which we do it automatically with individuals we know well, most of us are not used to doing it when we're speaking in public. The feeling of being on stage somehow suggests to our psyche that just as we are physically front and center, we must also be the center of the content, especially if we're brought in as an expert. However, speakers need an approach that lets them slip into the audience's shoes and connect with them as if they are people the speaker knows well.

Most busy professionals don't have 20 some years to learn this technique. That's why I've created a three-part system that is repeatable for making this connection. You can make your preparation, organization, and delivery all about your audience. I've been training others on this for years in a program I call Leaders Speak. People's results through this program have exceeded even my own high expectations. I have written this book to help even more people like you not just improve your public speaking, but also reach your listeners in ways that make a difference!

This could take you as little as 20 minutes!

Once you understand the basic process, the user-friendly strategies I explain shouldn't take much time. How quickly you are able to adapt to this new concept depends on your public speaking experience and your willingness to embrace the idea of making presenting about your audience instead of yourself. The more often you use it, the better and faster you will get at it, bringing it down to that 20-minute timing. Also, you can use an abbreviated version of this process when you are suddenly called on in a meeting or group to give an impromptu presentation.

Based on the Leaders Speak program, this book is broken up into three sections:

- Prepare for Your Audience
- Organize for Your Audience
- Deliver for Your Audience

Prepare for Your Audience
Part One, Chapters 1–6 will show you how to discover who will be in your audience, what is important to them, and what results they want that are different from how they currently work. You will learn how one manager changed her career by putting herself on the radar of the top executives at her company as a speaker and leader. You'll read about another speaker who turned her worst-case scenario into a potential teaching tool for overcoming fear. I've included numerous examples of how business

professionals improved their own results by helping their audiences improve theirs.

Organize for Your Audience

Part Two, Chapters 7–10 will teach you how to put ideas into a speech format based not only on your own information, but also on what the audience knows, values, and can use. Learn from my mistake what not to skip in every speech! See how you, too, can use a story to make a deep connection as one Fortune 200 company leader did. Find out what one sentence you can alter in your speech that will provide the quickest change with the most impact.

Deliver for Your Audience

Part Three, Chapters 11–15 will give you ways to make even your delivery match well with your audience in order for your preparation and organization efforts to come across the way you want them to so your audience can accept and apply your information. You will read about a sales rep for a nationally recognized ice cream brand who increased her volume so she could be heard. You will see how a CEO sidestepped a negative impression on television by smiling. You'll learn how practice really did make "better" for three speakers at an annual state kickoff meeting.

Action Items

At the end of every chapter, I've included Action Items that you can use to prepare, organize, and deliver to ensure that your next speech is all about

YOUR audience so you can change their lives and your own. Leaders Speak. Will you?

PART ONE:

Prepare for Your Audience

Chapters 1–6

"The only reason to give a speech is to change the world."

~ John F. Kennedy

Chapter 1 – Why Speak?

Why do public speaking? Why step up to the front of a room and put yourself out there? Why take the time, energy and effort to create and deliver presentations? Although there are many possible answers, it really boils down to two reasons.

- You can change audience members' lives.
- You can change your own.

<u>Change Audience Members' Lives</u>
We have all been members of an audience. We have seen leaders of organizations, cities, states and nations speak. Because we know that public speaking is something that leaders do, when we see anyone making a presentation, we naturally come to the conclusion that the speaker must be a leader of some kind. As audience members, most of us give leaders/speakers a certain degree of respect and attention, merely because they are in that role. As with leaders, when speakers are organized, knowledgeable, and care about their listeners, they have the power to change people's lives. Generally, lead-

ers who do not take into account the perspectives of their followers do not become as successful as those who do. It is the same with speakers. Most presenters have some knowledge and experience that led to their speaking, and most of them can organize their information into some reasonably ordered format. However, it is the speakers who are able to connect deeply with their audiences who utilize that power to its fullest.

It is this connection and not the basic information by itself that can change lives. Dynamic presenters can captivate audiences in the moment, highly intelligent leaders can impart wisdom during a speech, and speakers who do both can inspire people for a brief time. Then what? It is the results days, weeks, even years later that matter. You will make a difference if you get your audience to relate to, remember, and use the information and tools you've given them.

Think back to a time when you were in an audience and a speaker said something you've never forgotten. Picture a favorite teacher or mentor who prompted you to view yourself, your career, or the world in a new light. What have you done differently as a result of that person's influence? Your response to this question is how they changed your life. Here's an example of how mine was changed by a speaker.

When I began school at Concordia College in Moorhead, Minnesota, I started out as a math and computer science major. Although I had already been doing public speaking, it wasn't until my sophomore year that I discovered communications as a potential career option. I'm not sure how this would have happened if not for a teacher named Hank Tkachuk. In just one class, (similar to one speech), Hank said something about learning communication really being about learning people. I was sold. That resonated with me in a way no other phrase ever had. That idea transformed the class from simply part of a requirement to get a college degree into a passion I could spend the rest of my life doing. It caused me to sit down with Hank one on one to ask what types of jobs even exist in the communication industry. It led me to get a job in the Communication Department office, later become Hank's office assistant, decide to go into teaching, and ultimately do speaking and training through the business I run now. It gave me a way to spend my time and energy throughout my entire career serving others by doing things I already loved — learning people, adapting to their unique personalities, and helping them with their own communication. Although Hank had and still does have a profound effect on my career and life over many years of our continued relationship, it began with one statement in one speech.

You can do this as a speaker. Put yourself in that position so that your audiences will someday talk about you and the way you changed their lives. It is not as hard as you might think, it doesn't take as much time as you would guess, and it's a very repeatable process. This book will teach you how to do it.

Not everyone volunteers for leadership. Many people become leaders in their organizations because of sudden change, restructuring, or a timely need. In many circumstances, people have had no formal training and possibly no experience presenting. Suddenly, along with other leadership duties, they have to do public speaking. You expect leaders to speak and speakers to lead. In these cases, it is not merely an opportunity to help audiences, but a responsibility as well. And as you change the lives of others, you will find that your own life will also be changed.

Change Your Own Life
Whether you were speaking or leading first, once you've become a truly audience-oriented speaker, you will be asked to present more often. You will enjoy public speaking more as you gain confidence and realize that it was never about you, but instead about the audience who is listening. You will come to be viewed as an expert in your field. Increasingly, you will be sought after for both speaking and leadership, and you will be depended on to help others. This is how your own life will be changed. This will happen whether you are in a corporate setting or run a small business. Here are two examples of both these scenarios — how a manager in a large company and a small business owner changed their lives by improving their public speaking.

Corporate World:

Monika, a manager at Sprint, hired me to help her improve her speaking organization and delivery and become more confident at presenting. Her direct boss, peers, and the team who reported to her appreciated her intelligence, technical experience, and leadership. However, she did not have much visibility, if any, beyond her own employees, peers, and immediate director. When we started working together to strengthen her presentation skills, her boss's boss barely knew her name.

She did have some natural ability for public speaking. However, like most speakers, she would choose what information to cover and how to explain it by what she knew and found to be worthwhile points.

Monika came to understand through our sessions that the power of public speaking lies in making every speech completely about the audience. We went through the process together of digging into who will actually be there listening, what their perspective is on the project, the products, the timing, the results, and their "why" for showing up at the meeting. What are the audience members trying to accomplish? She saw that she could go through this process every time she would speak — it is easily repeatable. She grew more adept at sizing up her audiences quickly, understanding their wants and needs, and incorporating those into her main points, language, examples, and visuals.

Her audiences noticed. As she got better and better at connecting with her audiences, she was asked to speak to more groups. She began to be invited to present at more meetings, larger forums, to present to higher-level executives, and to present on behalf of Sprint externally. She continued to excel at her speaking because each time she would organize the content based on whether the audience was from Marketing, Production, Finance, a client company, a vendor company, executives or a mix of all of these. She has received vastly increased exposure and very positive feedback on her public speaking skills.

After 12 months of our coaching relationship, Monika now presents nine times more than she did before. She has been recognized by top executives as one of their trusted go-to leaders for her public speaking and for strategic thinking, initiative, and leadership in following through to completion of projects.

Monika said, "If I had been presenting to the CEO and senior management before learning this process, I would have been talking about schedules and details that aren't what they care about. Now instead, my mind immediately goes to what their bigger picture focus is — how this will affect our profitability, Sprint's reputation in the industry, and moving forward with our strategic vision." Learning to tailor her presentations to her audiences has changed the way they receive and use her information, thereby changing her career.

Small Business World:

Mark, owner of a small business called Miracles Through Water, joined a networking organization to get more clients. Although very personable, he was clearly uncomfortable when standing up to speak to a group. He spoke a little too fast, didn't speak loudly enough, and wanted to get it over with so he could get back in his chair (comfort zone). Therefore, it took more time for people to get to know him individually before they were able to learn about his vast knowledge, his excellent customer service, and all the benefits of his high-quality product. Although he was well liked by all who had gotten to know him, he hadn't received as much business from his networking efforts as he had hoped.

Then, Mark went through the Leaders Speak program, which is based on this book and consists of the same three parts: preparing, organizing and delivering for your audiences. He enjoyed it, improved quickly, and took it seriously. Because he came to believe strongly in the philosophy behind the whole process, he changed the way he thought. Before his speeches, he began asking himself why his topic, main points, and stories would matter to his particular audience. He would plan for them and organize his ideas for them, which built his confidence so that he could deliver at a volume and pace that matched their comfort levels.

The results have been noticeable to everyone who hears Mark speak. A few months after attending the workshops, he gave a speech in which he absolutely "knocked it out of the park" as they say. He received seven business referrals, five of which became clients, from that one presentation. Over the next few months, he got better and better at targeting his audiences, connecting with them and articulating how he could help them improve their health. Gradually, people hearing Mark present could clearly see his wonderful sense of humor, which had previously been stifled by his discomfort and rather choppy organization. He has transformed himself into a strong speaker and leader. Since going through the Leaders Speak program and applying the process, Mark has been elected president of his networking organization, speaks in public weekly, and has increased his income tenfold as a result!

Both Monika and Mark changed their careers through improving their public speaking. This is worth the risk, even though presenting can feel nerve-racking. This is the "why."

ACTION ITEMS – Chapter 1:

• Write down three benefits to your career that would be more likely to occur if you did more public speaking.

• Write down three audiences you could speak to in the next six months that could help your career, even if it's simply at fairly informal internal work meetings.

• Write down three topics that you could address that those audiences would benefit from hearing.

"Courage is not the absence of fear, but rather the judgment that something else is more important than fear."

~Ambrose Redmoon, writer

Chapter 2 – Fear Itself

Imagine yourself on a stage, looking out into a darkened room full of people who are waiting to hear you speak your first sentence. Will they care what you have to say? Will you forget your words?

If you've ever experienced these doubts, you are not alone. Most people get nervous when they have to speak in public, even those who do it often in their line of work. There's a reason that many people list public speaking as their number one fear, even ranking it higher than their fear of death. You expect to be evaluated, and you consider the stakes to include not just your credibility as a speaker, but also your overall credibility. Some people simply avoid these situations and the opportunities that go along with them. Others, such as Monika and Mark (discussed in the last chapter), decide the risk is worth taking because they can actually help people in their audience when they get past their own fear.

At a political dinner with about 200 people in attendance, I watched a United States Congressman take this risk. There were approximately seven speakers, but as the highest-level politician and keynote speaker for the event, this gentleman was the last to present. His nervousness leading up to his turn was evident. He was fidgeting, struggling to concentrate, and unable to focus on the speakers who preceded him. He would realize that the whole room was laughing at something a speaker said and would join in the chuckling a beat late. He kept attempting to put a natural smile on his face and nod when a speaker said something important. Clearly, the wait was excruciating for him. He was essentially missing what all the other presenters were saying, and was unable to enjoy the majority of the evening because of his own overwhelming anxiety. Ironically, when he stepped up to the microphone to speak, he looked much calmer, more comfortable and sincere. He was obviously well organized and actually gave a pretty smooth presentation. It is important to note that this was a group of his own political party, so he probably couldn't have faced a friendlier audience. Yet most of his night was spent in dread. The same is true for many people — the anticipation before speaking is the worst part.

Think about that for a minute. A United States Congressman, who is required to present, inspire and lead, gets nervous before public speaking and has to overcome his anxieties to do his work on a near-daily basis. How can he or anybody else overcome this natural anxiety? Is it possible to actually enjoy the moments leading up to a presentation and look forward to stepping up to the microphone? Yes, and you can begin by planning for your fear.

Throughout the 20 some years I've been in the communication field, I've seen countless examples of the fact that expectations are the biggest key to satisfying interactions with others. When we say things such as, "I didn't think this job would be like this," or "I didn't know marriage would be like that," we're describing times when things didn't occur according to what we had expected. Stephen Covey, author of *The 7 Habits of Highly Effective People* talks about the importance of expectations. He says, "The cause of almost all relationship difficulties is rooted in conflicting or ambiguous expectations around roles and goals." In public speaking, it matters what the audience is expecting of us (which we'll discuss in the next chapter) as well as what we expect of ourselves. Before presenting, many people expect to be nervous, therefore they are focusing on the negative from the start. We also sometimes anticipate that the audience will notice our anxiety, therefore increasing that feeling just by imagining it. If you are expecting yourself to be shaky or to fail in some way, you can increase the chances of one of those happening. Therefore, you've got to change your thinking and plan how to handle your fear. Admitting to yourself what you are expecting and consciously deciding to expect something different can change your outcome.

In this chapter, we will look at:

- Handling your worst-case scenario
- Increasing the likelihood of your best-case scenario

Handling Your Worst-case Scenario
What's the worst thing that could possibly happen?

Although this sounds negative, it can be very power-ful to specifically identify your worst-case scenario, face it and deal with it in advance. Much of what we fear, not just about public speaking but also in all of life, stems from the unknown. When we understand more about a person, a place, or a situation, we tend to fear it less. Although there are people who prefer speaking to strangers rather than peers because they care more what colleagues think, usually we reduce fear by reducing the unknown. This is why attempt-ing to know your audience, know your speech, and know your plan for handling the very worst thing you imagine has such an impact.

There are a number of factors that contribute to speakers' nervousness such as size of audience, status of listeners, and amount of pressure riding on the outcome. Notice that these issues, while increas-ing the feeling of risk, also increase the potential opportunity for great results. People also experience a variety of symptoms including sweaty palms, shaky voice, and difficulty breathing comfortably. When we assume control of what we can do about these, we don't feel as much like we are at the mercy of the situation or the other people involved or our own emotions. We can even experience a sense of calm or peace in this exercise, as did the speaker in the following example.

Let's look at the story of my client Kathleen, a Bob Proctor Life Success Consultant and professional speaker. When I asked Kathleen what would be the worst thing that could possibly happen to her while giving a speech, she told me that her worst fear was that her blood pressure would rise so high that her defibrillator would go off, knocking her physically to the ground.

The next logical question was: How likely is that? "Not very," she conceded. Her fear was magnified in her mind more than necessary, which is common. I then asked her what she would do if that actually did happen. "I guess I would just get up and tell the audience that my worst fear had just transpired and that I'm OK, showing them that you can move past your fears!" This woman speaks on the power of positive thinking and being the change you want to see in the world. She now recognizes that she can use her worst-case scenario as a teaching moment if it ever actually occurs. Because she has already faced it, she knows that her worst fear has now become even less likely to happen, and she has changed what she expects from herself and her speaking opportunity.

The three main actions Kathleen used can work for you as well. These are:

- Minimizing your irrational, built-up fears
- Deciding on a plan of action if your feared circumstance should come to pass
- Reducing the likelihood that your worst fear will occur

Kathleen, from a spiritual perspective, puts a tremendous amount of faith in God to guide her. She told me that she often prays right before speaking, asking God to not let her get too worked up, to not let her fall to the ground, and to just be with her. I suggested that she try thanking God for the nervousness and for the opportunity to help the people in the audience, and try praising God for however it goes and whatever the result. She immediately understood the difference between a somewhat desperate request that focuses on the very negative she wants to avoid and the freeing, trusting, other-oriented prayer that allows her to focus on her audience and the positive results that are possible.

Obviously, I understand that not all readers of this book will be spiritual themselves. To not make mention of it for those who are, though, would be an oversight. It's simply too great a part of dealing with fear for too many people to be left out of this chapter. The key thing I recommend to anybody, regardless of your spiritual beliefs, is to take the focus off of yourself. When you are truly putting yourself in the shoes of your audience, you will adjust your message, resulting in a much stronger connection that is felt by the audience and by you. And you will be less nervous!

Improving the Chances of Your Best-case Scenario
Now, what is the best thing that could possibly happen?

Whatever your answer, it is also your reason for facing your fear and taking that risk. What is more important than your fear? For Kathleen, her best case was that she would connect with her audience members, help them, and by doing so gain their trust. This ultimately would lead to them hiring her for coaching or mastermind groups. She now believes more than ever before that it will be worth moving past her fear and focusing on her audience every time she has an opportunity to show a group of people how she can help them move past their own fears.

What can you control to make your worst-case scenario less likely and your best-case scenario more likely to happen?

Realize that when you are in an audience yourself you don't completely condemn someone for being less than perfect. Remember that most audiences want you to do well and are rooting for you to succeed. Then, change your mindset. Remember that public speaking is not about you! It is always all about the audience. This is a very different way of thinking for many of us. We worry that everyone is watching us, judging us — how we look, sound, move. We take all the knowledge we have on a subject and organize it in a way that makes sense to us (if we bother to organize at all). Let me say this again. It is not about you!

Public speaking is all about the audience.

In the book, *Presentation Secrets of Steve Jobs*, he says the same thing, "During the planning phase of your presentation, always remember that it's not about you. It's about them." Although I agree, this is not true only during your planning, but at all stages along the way. We should consider the audience when we choose a topic, decide on main points, pick examples or stories to support our key ideas, organize the order of our thoughts, choose wording, pick visual aids, practice our presentation, and finally deliver our speech. It's not about what one speaker knows because that is already in a person's head. It is about picking the parts of what you know, which will resonate with your audience.

How do you know which information will matter to your audience? Well, how good are you at problem solving? Because that is exactly what public speaking is. How can you get this particular group of people information in a way they will understand it, relate to it, and even use it? That is your problem to solve. We all solve many different kinds of problems throughout our lives, and have developed techniques for succeeding at it. Think how you would describe your information to someone with whom you are completely comfortable. It would be a different explanation if you were talking to your parent, your friend, or the 3-year-old child in your life. You would adapt the story to that person's knowledge level, age, relationship to you, and other variables. Yet, when public speaking, we too often abandon this instinct, and prepare a presentation that does not account for the diverse backgrounds or perspectives of our audience. Instead we choose to see them as an anonymous group of strangers. This leaves the speaker feeling much more nervous than is necessary and the audience unsure how to relate to or use the information.

Most people in any kind of sales position probably do this adapting to their audience when selling to one or two people at a time, but can struggle when there are more listeners.

Every customer or client does not want or need the same things. Sales or marketing is essentially persuading. Outside of professional life, we do this adapting to others when we're trying to persuade someone in our personal life to agree with us or do something we want. Parents use diverse types of explaining or disciplining with different children because the same approach doesn't work with every child. Teachers sometimes vary their instruction methods because not every student has the same learning style. So we change our descriptions, pitches, and approaches to fit our audience of one person in just about every role in our lives.

The powerful part happens when we realize that we do this adapting and can apply it when there are more listeners. Then we can hone this skill and become better at it. This does not mean that the goal is to improve your ability to manipulate others. Although the result will often be positive for you, the point is to start by thinking of the other person's perspective. Put yourself in their shoes to empathize with them. If you go into an interaction sincerely considering what the other person's (or people's) wants are, your communication with them will be more effective. What is really driving them to be in this job, marriage or audience? Connect your information to their desires or goals and you will connect with them on a deeper level. Then they will be more likely to trust you and therefore more likely to listen to what you have to say and apply it within their own lives. When you can frame your thinking in this manner, your fear will be markedly decreased, as you will have largely forgotten about self. The more you focus on your audience, the less time and energy you have left with which to be self-conscious. Not only will your anxiety be reduced, you'll be better prepared to give a much more effective presentation. You now expect it to be about the audience.

Sometimes, people ask me if it's a good idea to tell your audience that you are nervous. I strongly recommend avoiding this. For one, audiences rarely see or are aware of the level of nervousness we feel in our own heads. During my 12 years of teaching public speaking at the college level, we videotaped all student speeches. One of the most surprising aspects to speakers was that the specific feedback they got from peers matched their video. They received comments on how good their eye contact was, how strong their voice was, or how confident they looked. The speakers could then see on their tapes that they really did look like that even though inside they felt it was completely obvious how anxious they were. The other more important reason not to call attention to your nervousness is that it brings the focus back to self. If you say something about your own fears, you're again making it about you and not about the audience, which can ultimately make you more nervous and can even turn off your audience at times. Your best bet is to truly put your energy toward how you can help the audience and attend to them.

Here's another piece of advice, especially for those of you who are reading this and already saying to yourself, "Oh no. I've done that. And that. I've been doing so many things wrong!"

Give yourself a break!

Many of the methods addressed in this book are included because they are used so often but aren't always the most effective. Don't dwell on the ghosts of speeches past. Even moving forward, once you've learned all this great stuff, there might be times when you revert to an old habit or make what you have come to consider a mistake. Is this the end of the world? No. I'm a professional speaker and I still make mistakes. Perfection should not even be the goal — not ever. It would interfere with our connecting with our audience, as they are not perfect either. Speakers and audiences alike are all human. When you know you've made a mistake, the simple fact that you are noticing something that you do not want to do is progress as long as you recognize it as such. It means you are on your way toward change. Instead of beating yourself up about it, pat yourself on the back for increasing your awareness of how you want to be even better. Maybe the next time you'll catch yourself in your head or during practice sessions and manage not to do it in your official speech. It takes time to alter habits that have been so engrained. And because so many of these less-effective behaviors are so common, when you can make a change, then you'll really stand out from other speakers.

Remember that not being too hard on yourself about the past, present and future can also increase the chances of your best-case scenario.

If prayer is part of your preparation, you could also try what I discussed in Kathleen's example earlier. If you pray by asking for God's results, not your own, and focusing on the audience (of one or many) instead of thinking of yourself, you will be amazed at the difference in your level of nervousness and your outcome. You've decided how you would handle your worst-case scenario and planned how to achieve your best-case scenario with your other-oriented mindset. Now, how do you know who will be in your audience?

ACTION ITEMS – Chapter 2:

• Write down your own worst-case scenario for what could happen when you get up to speak to an audience.

• Write down how you would handle that if it actually occurred.

• Write down what your best-case scenario is for what result could happen if you speak and do really well.

• Write down these words now and again before you speak to every audience, every time: It's not about me. It's about them.

"Seek first to understand, and then to be understood."

~ Stephen Covey, author

Chapter 3 – Know Your Audience

Think back to a time you were asked to speak to a particular group. Who asked you? I call that person your "gatekeeper." Often, you can find out a great deal of information about your audience from your gatekeeper. Analyzing your potential listeners is crucial to crafting a presentation in which you make it all about the audience. Considering who you expect to be there and what they are expecting from you and the topic can help reduce your uncertainty, thereby increasing your confidence. Some of the standard questions that journalists ask can also be a good start for you as a speaker. We'll go into detail on each of the following:

- Who will be there?
- What is the occasion?
- When will this speech take place?
- Where will the presentation take place?
- Why do your listeners want this speech/topic?

<u>Who Will Be There?</u>
Ask some basic questions to get broad ideas about your audience:

• Do they work for the same company?
• If so, which departments are represented?
• How big is the company?
• How many will likely be in the audience?
• Do they work in different companies but the same industry (such as sales)?
• Are they all part of the same association or organization (such as a chamber of commerce)?

Ask about demographics to start narrowing those ideas about your audience:

• Age range?
• Gender mix?
• Culture mix?
• Region of origin?
• Education and/or certification levels?
• Socio-economic levels?
• Employment levels (such as entry level to executive level)?

Ask about the general motivations of attendees:

• Is this required attendance?
• Is this expected attendance?
• Is this for certification/continuing education credits?
• Is this completely voluntary?

- Is this paid for by an organization?
- Is this audience paying some costs themselves?

What Is the Occasion?
Ask for specifics:

- Is this a celebration?
- Is this part of a longer/bigger event?
- Is this a conference?
- Is this an event that occurs regularly (such as annually)?

If you're speaking at any kind of awards or recognition event, you can assume that the environment is likely to be positive. If your presentation is part of a bigger occasion, you'll need to inquire about the other speakers and other topics and any themes that have been established. If you'll be speaking at a conference, you should check into the reason for the event, what the attendance is usually like and whether or not your session will be held concurrently with other sessions. If it is a regular occurrence, what is the history, purpose, and attitude toward the event?

When Will this Happen?
Ask how this could be timely for your audience:

- What is going on currently for this group?
- What has been happening recently?
- How long will you have?
- What time of day will it be?
- Will it be in addition to work or instead of work?

Current and recent for your audience:

Clearly, if you're doing a presentation for a large company that has just experienced layoffs, this will affect the current culture, tone and attitude of the group. The atmosphere might have been quite different if the event occurred before people lost their jobs. On the other hand, when a company has just had a hiring influx of new people who need to be trained, who need to learn the ropes, and who are unsure themselves as to the environment norms (unwritten rules), this group would also have a unique dynamic. Any major organizational change that the group has gone through recently will affect how your speech is received.

An organization once brought me in to speak on leadership to about 40 people from the middle management team. Timing was a challenge. They had just been through a major computer system upgrade. Unfortunately, the change was not handled well. This group of leaders had not been apprised of the change very far in advance; their opinions were not solicited and no one had communicated with them to explain what would be happening and when. My gatekeeper warned me in advance that at the time this was a disgruntled group, frustrated with upper management and therefore with anyone who was seen to be on management's side. So, she herself was riding the line of whether or not they trusted her and that could transfer to me as the speaker. Furthermore, she did not want the presentation to turn into a complaint session at which they would continue to vent about everything they had already been saying repeatedly, even though they were largely right. And, of course, she didn't want me to be bashing the administration either. This was, to date, the closest I've come to speaking to a potentially hostile audience. Personally, I was thrilled with the opportunity because audiences like this are in deeper need of assistance.

What can a speaker do about timing like this — when an audience is upset with good reason? If the group is on the defensive or even aggressive with a presenter who isn't involved in what has angered them, how can you handle this? Ask yourself what they want or need. What is important to them? Can you connect with their values or possibly even provide something that would be beneficial to them? Can you meet one or more of those needs?

This group needed:

- Appreciation
- Recognition
- Understanding
- Motivation toward a positive attitude
- Tools to lead and to meet these same needs for their employees

Although this is not word for word, this is basically how I began the presentation:

Here's what I believe about all of you. You work hard (appreciation). *You care about the [clients] you are helping, which is why you've honorably dedicated your careers to this profession* (recognition). *You are in the classic middle management squeeze where you don't get as much information or involvement as you would like, yet your own employees want you to keep them informed and involved. You don't always receive as much positive feedback as you'd like, yet you're expected to provide positive feedback to your own people without feeling like that example has necessarily been set. I know you've been through a particularly challenging computer change recently and you're frustrated* (understanding). *I'm impressed that you're here today because that shows that you want to be better than your situation and set a strong example as leaders. You can't control what happens above you, what your managers do. However, you can control what you do and how you communicate with the people who work for you. You can decide to adopt a positive attitude and spread that around among your own employees, fostering an open climate* (motivation). *That's what we're here to talk about today in this workshop — not the things we can't change, but the things that we can do, because I know you all want to be great leaders for your people!*

By the way, we essentially spent the rest of the time talking about the (tools) they could really use to lead their employees. During the first few minutes of introduction, you could actually see their physical presence change. Before the presentation began, on the whole, they were mostly tense and sitting stiffly in their chairs with an almost palpable edge to their attitude. One by one, as I said some simple, specifically sincere (this only works if you mean it) statements that addressed needs of theirs that weren't being met, they quite literally relaxed. Shoulders came down from their ears, postures sank back into more comfortable positions, fists opened, and jaws unclenched. Some people even smiled! The session went very well. The participants had great ideas, positive suggestions for each other, and a very enjoyable back and forth with me, including clearly appreciating the tools they were getting. If I had started by talking about myself and my qualifications or how I wanted this to be a productive session, it almost certainly would not have gone as well as it did. Starting by acknowledging the audience and the difficult spot the attendees were in, and empowering them to do something they could control, was likely the only way to break down the barriers. My presentation needed to be about them first before it could be about leading others.

Length:

Another factor to consider is length of the presentation. We are a scheduled society, so always stick to the amount of time you're given or slightly less. If it is likely that the audience will have questions and you want to take those in a group setting, then you need to leave time for them. If you plan to have attendees do activities on their own or request their participation, you must allow for this in your allotted time. Tell the audience how much time they've got for each question or activity, which will help them and you. If you're doing more than a two hour session, you'll probably need to take a break somewhere in the middle. Also, you should think about soliciting more input and participation from the audience if the session goes longer than a couple of hours. People's attention spans aren't naturally that long, so getting them involved can make the session seem to go faster and be more effective. Many people consider time to be a respect issue, so always start and finish on schedule.

Time of day:

If you are speaking first thing in the morning, it's a good idea to either bring coffee and tea or ask if it will be provided. If your presentation includes a meal, know that it will provide competition for you. People will look at their food and have a little less eye contact with you. It can also be harder for audience members to keep from chatting with each other while eating, so consider breaking for the meal and letting that serve as a time for networking or one of your small group activities if that's an option.

During or outside of work:

As far as whether the session is during or after work hours, this aspect can vary. Some people will prefer that a presentation be offered during the workday because anything outside of that is their own time. However, others feel that if they have to take time away from work, they're more stressed about what they are not getting done, whereas outside of work, it's a choice that they want to make and can look forward to it. This depends largely on the topic and the level of interest in it. If people are truly excited about the subject, they are obviously more likely to appreciate the opportunity to attend either during or outside of work hours. Besides when, it also matters where the session is held.

<u>Where Will this Take Place?</u>
Ask if there is any significance to the location:

- Is this at the group's work place?
- Is it a regular meeting place?
- Is it accessible to all, including clear directions?
- Is it convenient to all, including aspects such as parking?
- Are there any positive or negative associations with location?
- Will there be distractions?
- What is the room size?
- What is the room shape?
- Who will manage the audio system?

- Is there PowerPoint ability?
- Will there be separate chairs or tables (round or rectangle)?
- Will the layout be theater-style or classroom?

Why Are You Giving this Speech or Presenting this Topic in the First Place?

- Does the leader want this topic?
- Does the group want this topic?
- Is there a reason the group needs this training?
- Is this part of a regular, ongoing education initiative to keep skills sharp?
- If it is ongoing, what other topics have been covered recently?
- Why did the decision makers choose you to do this?
- What are the audience members' goals?
- What results do they want and expect from the session?

Again, as you will read throughout this book, this mindset is not solely for people standing on a stage with a microphone. Any time you are reporting during a meeting, on a conference call with a group, or explaining to your clients how or why they can use your services, you should figure out the answer to these basic questions about your audience – who, what, when, where and why, even if there will only be one person listening.

ACTION ITEMS – Chapter 3:

• Write down the answers to at least a couple of the "Who" questions about an audience you will speak to or could speak to at some point.

• Write down the answers to at least a couple of the "What" questions about an occasion or event where you know you'll speak or could.

• Write down the answers to at least a couple of the "When" questions about a definite or likely audience's timing – when they usually bring in speakers.

• Write down the answers to at least a couple of the "Where" questions about a certain or possible audience's locations – where they hold meetings.

• Write down the answers to at least a couple of the "Why" questions – if an audience did have you speak, why they would want you and your topic.

"Understanding can overcome any situation, however mysterious or insurmountable it may appear to be."

~ Norman Vincent Peale, author

Chapter 4 – Seeing Through Their Eyes

We often think we know best about what an audience needs. We are the experts in our subject matter — that's why we were asked to speak, right? Probably, but our content is not usually going to be enough on its own. We've got to clearly demonstrate to the audience why and how the information matters to them. It's not even sufficient to think, "What would I want to know if I were in the audience?" That's a good start, but you need to go further and think of what this specific audience might be hoping to hear or interested in knowing. This is not the same as telling them only what they want to hear. You must come at your topic from their perspective to connect with them before you can challenge them to change their lives.

Ask yourself:

• What <u>beliefs</u> do they care about most?
• What <u>attitudes</u> are important to them?
• What <u>values</u> are deeply rooted for them, priorities that transcend many situations?

- What experiences have affected their lives?
- What identities or descriptions do they use for themselves?

There's a phrase that I like in some public speaking textbooks called "frame of reference." This is where people are coming from, so to speak. Imagine each audience member with a large, empty picture frame in their hands, holding the frame up in front of their faces. Every piece of information we give them, be it a main point, story, statistic, whatever, will go through that frame to get to them. That framework is made up of all their beliefs, attitudes, values, and experiences, all of which usually factor into their identities. If what you say fits easily along with those things, they are more likely to agree with you and even act on what you say. However, if your information conflicts with any part of their own frame of reference, then it will become harder to reach them or convince them of anything, including hiring you.

Of course, the difficult part is that each individual has a different frame of reference, and you probably won't know all the components of anyone's framework. If you try to sell horseback riding lessons to someone who loved horses growing up, it will likely be easier to connect with her. On the other hand, if you try to sell that same idea to someone who fell off a horse when he was young and got hurt, it will be a tougher sell. That person's experience has affected his view or attitude on the whole industry negatively, and what you're saying is not consistent with his own frame of reference.

If you have the opportunity to conduct a survey of your audience prior to your speaking engagement, always do so. If not, you'll have to rely on your gatekeeper and use some generalizations about the type of people who work for a certain industry or company. For many people, this might sound like a horrible idea at first. Aren't you supposed to avoid stereotyping and painting whole groups with one brush? Yes, but you have to start somewhere and this is done with positive intentions, not to condemn, but rather to appreciate your audience. The more you can find out about an organization, the more you can imagine what many audience members might share in their frames of reference. For instance, if you know that you're speaking to an accounting firm, you can probably assume that they will want numbers, statistics, evidence, and analysis based on data. If you only have emotional stories, feeling statements and heartfelt pleas, you'll be unlikely to connect with them as well.

You should never use all logical or all emotional appeals because you can't assume that every audience member will fit the mold, but you can lean in one direction based on what you can surmise about a particular group. People often consider part of their identity to be what they do for their work — I am an engineer, a baker, a bank manager, a stay-at-home mom, a computer analyst and such. How they would describe themselves is a big part of their frame of reference because they view the world through that identity. If you're communicating with an audience of one, this becomes easier to pinpoint.

When teaching college, I once had a night class with a mix of traditional and nontraditional students. A very pleasant woman who took my Public Speaking course ended up telling our class at the end of the semester that the frame of reference concept had been practically life changing for her. Although she was pretty comfortable standing up front, speaking to public audiences, she and her teenage daughter clashed fairly often. So for her, that audience of one was tougher than most groups. When she realized that her daughter's frame of reference and her own were almost exactly opposite, it helped her understand their relationship and feel better about it, even though nothing but that awareness had changed. Her daughter thought she could be independent; she herself thought it was her responsibility to take care of her daughter (beliefs). Her daughter wanted to be trusted to make decisions; she wanted to guide her daughter to avoid mistakes (values). Her daughter viewed trying new things as good and liked discovering things for herself; she considered protecting her daughter from failure to be positive (attitudes). They perceived and reacted to every occurrence differently (experience). Every one of their top priority areas was like this, completely opposing. They could not each have their most important needs met concurrently.

My student realized that her daughter wasn't trying to disrespect her or meaning to push her buttons, she just had totally different motives and wants as a teen, than my student did as a mother (identity). She ended up telling her daughter that she would keep caring, advising and protecting because that was her role as a mom, but that she would respect that the daughter had her own role and frame of reference and the two would not always mesh eas-

ily. Her daughter truly appreciated this attitude change in her mother (which means her mother managed to alter her own frame of reference at least a little bit). My student considered this a huge breakthrough in their relationship and could tell that it had already improved the overall satisfaction for both of them.

Remember that lives can be changed no matter how many people are in the audience. This approach can work in all your communication interactions if you really use it. Here's how one general presentation topic could be changed based on at least three different audiences.

From a public speaking standpoint, my client Jackie, who was fighting a battle against Stage 4 cancer, had written a book, "Surviving Cancer 101." She was speaking in public about handling the disease. In our Leaders Speak program, Jackie realized that she would need to be talking about very different concepts depending on her audience. Current cancer patients are often exhausted, fearful, hopeful and pressured to be "strong" for their supporters. Depending on their diagnosis, treatment and prognosis, they may need or want very different information even though they may all be fighting the same disease. Supporters of patients can feel powerless, uncertain as to how best to help, and go through their own sadness for those they love. Cancer survivors are usually interested in moving on, helping others, embracing life and appreciating how they were changed by their experience. Commonly, audiences would include a mix of all these perspectives.

Jackie herself felt that it was much more difficult when she was a supporter in her mother's cancer fight than when she was on her own journey as a patient. As if accommodating all those views is not a tall enough order, when Jackie imagined talking to doctors, she realized how extremely varied her approach might need to be. She believes strongly in holistic methods of healing (along with medical treatments) that much of the health care community does not always favor. She would have the challenging opportunity to appeal to the physicians' desire to help patients heal and to save lives in order to convince them that nontraditional treatments also have merit.

You can adapt to your audiences or parts of your audience with your main point choices, your wording, your examples, your visual aids, and even your delivery. When you can compliment your audience sincerely, you are letting them know that you understand their perspective.

When Continental Title Company hired me to conduct a workshop for their partners, clients and potential clients, I was able to start by commending them on their leadership. The audience of realtors, mortgage brokers and title representatives appreciated the fact that I acknowledged their roles as leading people through some of the toughest challenges of their lives — moving to a new city, finding a new house, choosing a good neighborhood and making a home in the community for themselves and their families. Those are high stakes, usually accompanied by at least some stress. These real estate folks are the people who lead their clients to make solid decisions.

Once you have analyzed your audience, of one or many, and understand their beliefs, attitudes, values, experiences and identities, you can then try to assess how your audience's frames of reference might be similar to each other's and to your own.

ACTION ITEMS – Chapter 4:

• Write down at least three values that you believe the majority of your audience considers important to them.

• Write down at least three experiences that you believe most of your audience has had, especially any that are recent for their industry.

• Write down at least three words that you believe would describe who the people in this audience are — personality types, characteristics they have in common with each other.

"We cannot live only for ourselves. A thousand fibers connect us with our fellow men."

~ Herman Melville, author

Chapter 5 – Common Ground

At this point, you need to go back to self for a few minutes. However, you'll see that the reason for it is ultimately about the audience yet again. Think of your natural strengths — the positive personality descriptors that most people who know you would say you simply are, without even having to try. These are usually also your strengths as a speaker.

There is tremendous value in writing down what is in your mind so that you can see it visually, react to it, and go back to it for future use. Anyone who has had training in goal setting has heard this before. For this purpose, you'll be asked to draft several quick lists throughout this process to reach your result of deeply connecting with your audiences. Do not dismiss this exercise as too much work. You might only need five to 10 items and five to 10 minutes for each list. This chapter will get you going with your first three lists and you will find examples of each list at the end of the chapter. There is also a section at the end of the book with all the list examples in a row.

List #1 – Yourself
List #2 – Your audience (If you completed Action
    Items from Chapter 4, you can use those.)
List #3 – Your common ground

List #1 – Yourself (See an example at the end of this chapter.)

First, jot down what you know about yourself as a person and a professional. Include your strengths, priorities, goals, challenges and successes, but also include at least seven personality descriptions.

List #2 – Your Audience (See an example at the end of this chapter.)

Second, if you haven't been doing so, you'll want to go ahead and write down what you think your audience values, what they are like, and their descriptions. What do they care about most? What are their goals? Make an actual list if you didn't while reading the last chapters, which will become List #2. Use at least seven words or phrases. If you completed the Action Items at the end of Chapter 4 and have at least seven, then you have the first part of this list done. Now, go back through that list and ask yourself about each word: If I know that, what else do I know? So, if you know they are business owners, maybe you put "busy." What else do you know about people who are busy? They get "stressed." Go one more level. If you know they are stressed, what else do you know? They feel "rushed." If you'll take the seven words about your audience and go two more levels, you will be going deeper than most other speakers. This gives you more options for ways to observe how you may be similar to your audience. It also helps you see things that, even if you don't have them in common with your audience, are major factors that the audience members have in common with each other and therefore could be helpful to acknowledge.

A client, Robin, who sells health products, was speaking to firefighters. Although she did not have this aspect in her work, she recognized that the firefighters were like each other in that they risk their lives for the safety of others in their communities. She complimented them on that specific characteristic of bravery and connected it to the, albeit much less dramatic, notion that she is also trying to save people's lives through increased health, which can be a particular challenge for folks who work around smoke. She took something that wouldn't appear to be a similarity with her audience and still made a connection with it.

<u>List #3 – Your Common Ground (See an example at the end of this chapter.)</u>
Your third list will be easy if you have many items that are on both List #1 and List #2. Circle them and transfer them to a new List #3. The reason this is important is that we tend to like people with whom we have something in common. People will say that business is just that — business. It's not personal.

Here's the problem with that thinking: It is fairly unusual to say, "I can't stand this guy, but I keep hiring him because he's so good at what he does." That might happen here and there, but not very often. We tend to hire people we trust. We tend to trust people we like. So, if we don't get to them liking us, we've got less chance of getting all the way to them hiring us. Because we often tend to like those who are similar to us, establishing commonality becomes a crucial step in connecting with our audience of one or many.

Dr. Ivan Misner, the founder of Business Network International (BNI) says, "All things being equal, we hire our friends. Most of the time, all things not being equal, we still hire our friends." Stop and think for a moment about whether you've practiced this. If not, it is still good to know that many people operate this way. If so, then yourself are another example of business being personal.

You might think this whole idea could be challenging if you don't really have much in common with your audience. However, when you take a broad approach, we're all human beings with some basic drives, so we should have something similar on which to connect. We essentially all want understanding, respect, and success. Those don't always look or sound the same for each individual, but they are root desires that most people want in both their business and personal arenas. If you don't have many items on both your List #1 and the audience's List #2, then start with the following questions to generate List #3 – Your common ground.

- Do you and the audience hold any similar values?
- Do you experience any like challenges?
- Are your worlds similar, even indirectly?
- What else does that tell you about them?
- How can you be more specific?

Sharing values can be key because of their importance. Values tend to be things we almost always hold in high regard such as honesty, integrity, service, respect, care for family, faith, health, finances, or open communication. However, if there aren't many overlapping aspects on those lists, then go to a more basic list as discussed in the last chapter about what generalizations you can make about this audience. Now look again to see if any of those ideas are ones that match your list.

After values, it can be helpful to realize that you and your audience go through some of the same kinds of struggles. Start again with basic, general ideas such as the economy, industry cycles, roles of business owners, the need to close in sales, hiring quality employees, and having to prioritize what marketing dollars to spend where. By taking a general approach to get started, you'll find some things that you likely have in common with your audience. You can be more specific later and going two extra levels deeper on each word will help.

Do your world and their world share any experiences? For example, most companies have to do some type of sales, marketing, bookkeeping, human resources, planning, strategy, and customer service. So, if you are willing to open your mind to a wide enough view, you should at least have somewhere to begin. Then, once you've gotten some answers, even if they're generalizations, you can try to dig deeper to get more specific details by asking what else each of those answers probably tells you.

A client, Karen, who is a life coach, was planning to conduct a workshop on the Myers-Briggs assessment tool. (This is a tool to help people better understand personality types, and the results are depicted by four letters, i.e., ENFJ or ISTP.) Karen was going to be doing this presentation through the University of Missouri Kansas City, but it was open to the entire Kansas City community, not just those on campus. She literally had no idea who would be attending. Although a certified expert in her field with a vast knowledge of the subject, Karen was uncertain how best to put together the workshop, how much to cover, how much detail to use, how much to have the participants do for this initial session, etc. The reason for this challenge in getting started was likely due to the lack of information as to who would be in her audience. Therefore, we began by discussing: Who cares? Not in a sarcastic way, but literally. Who would be drawn to this information? Who tends to be interested in this sort of topic? How has it been marketed (what drew them in and what will they expect)?

We wrote down what we thought we could assume about people who would value this type of workshop enough to pay for it and spend time attending. They would likely be self aware, reflective, open minded, and intelligent. Karen herself is all these things naturally, without trying. This means that not only does she share these traits with her likely audience members, but they are also strengths of hers and probably of theirs. They probably have at least one relationship in mind that could benefit from the information. They might have a desire to act on or change something in their own behavior based on their results. They probably view personality assessments as positive, worthwhile, even fun, as does Karen. They might be in education, psychology, sociology, counseling or coaching fields, as is Karen.

Because we knew it was being promoted locally, the audience members would also be primarily local. We discussed what we assume about people in Kansas City. Although we think of stereotyping as negative, again it can be helpful if you have very little certain knowledge of the attendees. We jotted down characteristics that residents of Kansas City might share such as hard working, down to earth, friendly, hearty, cultured and kind. Karen also has all these things in common with her probable audience.

Assuming these traits about the audience, then we could take all the wonderful information Karen has to impart and organize it according to the people who would likely be there. We decided she could ask at the start what brought people there. This way she could quickly confirm her educated guesses and immediately get more specific than her advance plans. Then she could ask if people have taken the assessment before and how they've used it or if they haven't taken it before, how they think they could use it. She could give an example showing them how she herself has used it to establish that common bond and show that they have some similarities. In Karen's case, this helps them trust her not only because she is like them, but also because she is putting her own vulnerability out there by trusting them with her own example.

Remember trust is reciprocal. Audiences trust speakers who are willing to trust them by sharing personal information. People who are interested in personality analysis may use it professionally and those who are hard working and down to earth (like Karen) would appreciate this start because it would heighten the value they would receive from attending. Having asked them at the start, she would know how much detail to include in her overview of the assessment; then she could have them give examples of challenges in relationships, then give her own examples of how the assessment can help with those struggles to produce results different from what they might have been frustrated by in the past.

Hang onto your first three lists — yourself, your audience and your common ground lists — so you can refer back to them later in the process.

ACTION ITEMS – Chapter 5:

• Write down your List #1 about Yourself.

• Write down your List #2 about Your Audience, starting with your answers from Chapter 4 Action Items and taking at least five of those words or phrases two levels deeper asking yourself what else each word tells you that you also probably know about this audience.

• Write down your List #3 about Your Common Ground, basically writing anything that was on your - List #1 and your audience - List #2, including the deeper level terms so you can visually see at a glance what similarities you have with your audience.

See List Examples on the next pages to show you how to make your own lists.

LIST EXAMPLES

List #1 – Yourself

Client: Lisa, Founder and Chairwoman of the Board for Safe Place for Kids

* = Top 3 Most Defining – If you could only use 3 words, what would they be?

Compassionate
Friendly
* Energetic
Organized
Confident
Thorough
* Passionate
Supportive
Innovative
* Appreciative

<u>List #2 – Your Audience</u> – going to a 2nd and then 3rd level of depth

Client: Lisa, Safe Place for Kids

Audience: Northland Chamber of Commerce

⬭ = Also on List #1 – Yourself

If we know these:	We also know these:	And also know these:
Level#1	Level #2	Level #3
- Involved	- Care	- Compassionate
- Busy	- Limited time	- Stressed
- Political	- Agendas	- Accomplished
- Tight knit	- Know others	- Loyal
- Passionate	- Energetic	- Confident
- Community	- Protective	- Like a family
- Supportive	- Giving	- Generous
- Organized	- Structured	- Thorough
- Growth	- Ambitious	- Promoting
- Leaders	- Responsible	- High standards

List #3 – Your Common Ground

Client: Lisa, Safe Place for Kids

Audience: Northland Chamber of Commerce

From 1st level	From 2nd	From 3rd
- Passionate	- Energetic	- Compassionate
- Supportive		- Confident
- Organized		- Thorough

"Time and money spent in helping men to do more for themselves is far better than mere giving."

~ Henry Ford, Founder of Ford Motor Company

Chapter 6 – Results, Results, Results!

Whether your audience is from your own organization, potential clients, an industry group at a conference, or a group of community members, the listeners will want to hear what will help them reach their own goals. Unless you're speaking from a personal standpoint at a wedding or a church gathering, something that is not task related, people expect there to be some outcome from your speech that they can use to improve their own results.

Results are why we do such an in-depth audience analysis. Although most of us know that with any type of sales pitch we should connect what we have to what the audience needs, we don't always know how to do it, and we don't usually go deep enough for it to really make a difference. We might refer to all being from Kansas City or something surface without mentioning what that can specifically mean. Just as with the example with Karen from the last chapter, when we can connect on a deeper level such as strengths, an aspect of which an audience is somewhat proud, that will matter. When you have the access, ask your audience how they measure results so that you know you are on target with what they care about most. When that is not an option, do your best in advance to make some educated guesses based on your analysis of them. When you first begin your speech, ask them to answer your questions if you have room in your time limit. Don't worry about having come to "wrong" conclusions and then having to change some of the content you prepared. It's better to find out early on how to adapt, rather than sticking to your plan and missing the mark.

You might think if you do not have specifics available to you that what results people are hoping for could vary quite widely. However, it's fairly safe to assume there are a few essential areas in which people want to improve results, even when their current results are already relatively good. Individuals from all walks of life tend to care about five things: their loved ones, their health, their finances, their time, and their work. This sounds like an over-simplification. What about religion, travel, community and many other things that people value? I'm not saying that people only care about the aforementioned aspects, but the point is almost everyone cares about at least these five things. Religion can be a part of spiritual health for many while travel can fall under finances and how we spend our time. Community is often an extension of caring for our loved ones, so those two are really the same item.

Here are the basic priorities for almost everyone:

- Family safety
- Better physical, emotional and spiritual health
- More money
- More time
- More success at work

Any time you can help people in these five categories, they will usually be quite interested and will therefore be more likely to connect to the rest of your message. By the same token, when you can take away their pain in any of these areas, making things easier for them, you will win them over almost every time. As I've emphasized before, the better you know your audience, the more specifically you can address their priorities or pains. People tend to set goals around these five topics, so consider how to help them reach or exceed those results. The more specific your comments and examples, the stronger your connection will be. The stronger your connection to your audience, the more likely it is they will listen, like, trust and ultimately hire you!

People have occasionally asked me if I am a motivational speaker. I usually say no, that's not what I call myself. The reality is that anyone who is good at public speaking will be motivational. Unfortunately, too often the connotation that goes with that is that the content of a motivational speech is fluff. It is crucial to provide audience members and clients with concrete information and tools that they can immediately use when they return to their own work or life to increase their own results. Every time you achieve this goal, a side effect is that people are motivated to use those tools. It is a natural outcome as opposed to a primary purpose. When we receive really good training on anything — a job, an aspect of a job, a project, or a presentation, we want to work on it because now we know how and are confident in getting started, which is often the hardest part for many of us.

Presenters of all kinds — on a stage to a formal audience, around a conference room table at a meeting, or in your office with a potential client — should use value statements that highlight the benefits that person or group (audience) will experience from listening to you and through working with you. Let's look at some examples of this for each of our five essential common results areas.

Example 1 – Family safety: A client of mine, Scott, started his own roofing business, Christian Brothers Roofing, with the express purpose of providing an often necessary service with integrity, including Christian values. He was advertising on a local Kansas City Christian radio station, but his commercial did not indicate specifically that his business was a Christian company. Scott asked me to analyze his ad and then to write and direct a new one for him. His original ad didn't mention his own Christianity and began with his own name, "I'm Scott Horstmann..." and had more "I" statements than "you" statements related to the listeners. Because Scott's core values were similar to those of his audience, we changed his ad to state that his organization is faith-based. Because the most crucial reason for needing a reliable roof is to protect the family members in the house, we appealed to people's desire to keep their loved ones safe. Scott addressed the roofing results that would matter most to his audience members. As to Scott's own results, his calls per week more than doubled in the first 30 days after changing his radio ad to this wording.

> *What are the most important things under _your_ roof? For you, those might be family members, furniture pieces or other precious memories. Well, I'm Scott Horstmann. I own Christian Brothers Roofing where we are striving to glorify God through helping people like you protect your dearest belongings.*
> *If you're going to trust the roof over your head, you need to be able to trust your roofing company. With Christian Brothers, you get years of experience and integrity.*
> *Don't wait until you _know_ there's a problem. Call us today for a complimentary 16-point roof and gutter inspection at Christian Brothers at 816-453-ROOF or visit our website at 453ROOF.com!*

Example 2 – Better health: My client and massage therapist, Mandy, actually incorporated this into her company name, Hands on Healing. Mandy was putting together a podcast that had a very wide, potential audience. She originally wrote a speech explaining what she offers, but together we changed her approach to target the results clients want to gain from her services. In her case, we were able to give examples of her past clients who literally had results of Mandy relieving their pain! Usually, that's more metaphorical. One of her clients had daily back pain for years, and after just one session with Mandy, her pain was gone. When Mandy followed up a couple of days later, her client said that her back did not hurt anymore and that she couldn't remember the last time she had been without pain. Mandy checked again a few weeks later and found out that her client was still doing well. Another of Mandy's clients had chronic migraines that changed through working together for seven to 10 regular sessions. As a result, instead of daily, debilitating migraines, her client experienced only one or two per week and they were much more manageable. Giving examples of success stories that specifically describe other people's results is often a great strategy to use because listeners can picture a specific story and imagine getting those results themselves.

Example 3 – More money: My client and financial adviser, John, is a CPA and author of the book, *How to Build Tax-Free Wealth*, which focuses on Roth IRAs. He sometimes offers free seminars on topics such as planning for retirement. John explains to people that one advantage of working with him instead of many other investment counselors is that he can also advise them on the tax implications of their decisions. A large number of his competitors are not CPAs. Some audience members at one of John's presentations were greatly impressed and relieved that he was not suggesting (as so many competitors do) they check also with their tax adviser. These people expressed frustration at having spent time and money with their prior financial professional, only to be told to go spend more money and schedule yet another meeting with someone else. John pointed out that some financial advisers suggest a certain type of investment, but due to the tax implications, that investment would only be good for a small percent of the population. So, for most people, not only would that choice not make them money, but could cost them money in taxes. The problem is that many advisers do not know the tax laws. When your whole business is maximizing people's money, it is invaluable to offer an immediate money-saving strategy that saves time as well!

Example 4 – More time: My client, John, CEO of a student services company, speaks in different regions across the nation. He came to me because there were about to be some significant and complex changes across his industry. He wanted to help his clients really understand the differences. Not only did we make a point to do that, but we also geared all his information even more toward his audiences. We purposely structured his speeches around the benefits of hiring his company, such as saving people time. His organization exists to aid higher education institutions in tracking and collecting debt from student loans. This allows his clients to do the jobs they want and need to do instead of spending up to 40 hours a week to do a thorough job of it internally. John emphasizes that this is a conservative estimate of the time he saves schools because employee(s) would also need to be trained in how to accurately and effectively perform these responsibilities. John was so satisfied with his ability to improve his own presenting that he later sent one of his managers, who spoke around the country for his organization, to work with me to strengthen her skills.

Example 5 – More success: A colleague who attended one of my trainings on networking, Kristina, was an executive with a card printing company. She was trying to create a variety of presentations she could use to explain what she does to her networking group so they could in turn explain it to others to send her referrals. We examined how she could tell the audience what results they could get from using her product, and another audience member in the training session told Kristina a success story from using her company. A promotional products company had sent out "thank you for your business" cards. Specifically in response to those cards, that company did more than $8,000 of business during the next 30 days. So we incorporated that story into her presentation. Kristina used that example the following week with her networking group and her own result was that she got twice the number of referrals in one day than she had ever had before.

Put yourself in the audience's position. If you spend an hour, half a day or a whole day at a presentation or a workshop, do you want to think that you've gotten interesting information? Or do you want to walk away with tools that you can actually start using immediately to make your own family, health, time, finances and work even better than they already are? Therefore, when you're the speaker, do everything you can in your own presentations (to one client at a time or groups of many people) to clearly connect your information to your audience's goals and their potential results! Use the general areas of family, health, money, time and work success, and then be as specific as you can for your audience. One of the most effective ways to do this is by making the focal points of your speech more oriented toward the audience. This brings us to the actual crafting of the speech.

ACTION ITEMS – Chapter 6:

•   Write down at least three challenges that you know or think that your audience likely has. These can be general such as "make more money" but be as specific as you can.

•   Write down at least three results (or changes) you believe your audience would like to see along the lines of those challenges — again, more specific is more beneficial.

•   Write down at least three ways or tools with which you can help them make those changes or reach those results.

PART TWO:

Organize for Your Audience

Chapters 7–10

"If you have an important point to make, don't try to be subtle or clever. Use a pile driver. Hit the point once. Then come back and hit it again. Then hit it a third time — a tremendous whack!"

~ Winston Churchill

Chapter 7 – Choose Main Ideas for Audience

You sit down to write your speech. Maybe you write something and then erase it just like Tom Hanks' character did when he was writing an e-mail to Meg Ryan's character in the movie "You've Got Mail." You realize that this is how you felt back in school, trying to begin assignments but instead finding yourself staring at a blank paper or screen (depending on your generation). Either way, for most of you, the hardest part was and is simply getting started. So, you decide to do other things first. You clean up your place, shop, make phone calls, do filing, and spend time with your family or friends. Hey, those things also needed to be done, so why not? The truth is, you're procrastinating. You are assuming that when you've cleared those other things off your plate, then you will be able to focus on your speech. However, here's the problem with that approach. When you resume work and go back to the presentation, the only thing that has changed is that you now have less time to prepare and complete the task. Sometimes this means that you force yourself to write something down simply because you're running out of time. Unfortunately, this hurried and last minute work is often evident in your writing or speaking. You may start writing just to get something down, but it is stiff and you don't know where you're going with it because you have no plan. And sometimes, especially if it's a speech, not a paper, you decide to wing it! Maybe it even goes pretty well, and you decide next time to skip the excruciating process of even pretending you're going to write something like an outline or notes. You don't need to, you can just wing it again and again and again.

Folks who tend to wing it, congratulations. Most likely, you have some natural public speaking ability. However, you can utilize that talent more effectively when presenting if you learn how to plan for your speech. This planning doesn't have to be a long or painful process. The main problem is that you want to start at the beginning, which would seem to make sense. However, the start is the introduction. Until you've written the bulk of the speech, you don't yet know what you are introducing. Therefore, you need to skip the introduction and not start with the first lines. You need to begin with the main points by making two more lists. (At the end of this chapter, there will be examples of these lists to help you get organized. And at the end of the book, there is a section with all five of the list examples.)

This chapter will explain three aspects:

List #4 – Your Priorities
List #5 – Audience Priorities
Strength in Vulnerability

Some people will say that you should have already had a purpose in mind before doing the preparations you've done up to this point. For instance, if you were given a general topic, you should have decided going into your preparation what the goal of your speech is (i.e., to inform on how to build a client base). However, I disagree with this approach and believe that you should wait. If, in your list making, you recognize the primary reason the audience is coming to hear you speak, then you should try to make that purpose yours. What if you thought your subject should be about getting more clients but the listeners would prefer to get more purchases from the clients they already have? Remember that you're supposed to be gearing everything toward the audience's desired results. If it is not feasible to make both the same, then try to incorporate the listeners' goals as much as possible into your own. For instance, there is a very different feel to your audience if your goal is to sell listeners something than if you help them reach their own goal of increasing their number of services per client, therefore making your goal about them.

<u>List #4 – Your Priorities (See an example at the end of this chapter.)</u>
For this part, you should have your List #2 - Your Audience and List #3 - Your Common Ground handy so you can use them. Next, if you do not already have in mind the major categories of information you want to cover (and you really shouldn't), then get ready to make another list. This is one of the only instances when I'll suggest for you to be selfish. Do not be concerned about who will attend this speech. Jot down all the points that you could talk about on the subject of your presentation. Don't worry about how important or big or small they are, just get down a fairly long list of 15 to 25 items. Then, put a star by the three to five items that you believe are the most important to you to include in your speech. If you could only use three to five sentences, what would they be?

<u>List #5 – Audience Priorities (See an example at the end of this chapter.)</u>
Now, go back to Your Audience List #2. Who will be there or who will likely attend? What might they want to learn that would likely make an impact on their own results? On List #4 that you just created, circle the three to five items from the entire list that you believe that particular audience will find most important and transfer them to a new List #5 for the sake of the visual focus on the audience. (Sometimes, you might also be inspired by words on the list of things you have in common with your audi-

ence.) Really use the earlier list on what you know about your audience to consider this from their point of view. As I've said before, it is not quite enough to think, "What would I want to hear if I were in the audience?" It is much better to ask, "What will they want to hear because they will be in the audience?" Remember, it's all your information that you already know and can explain and use. You won't end up outside of your area of expertise because you have the information. Now you're making it about the audience. Of everything you know about this subject, you have just identified the points the audience will care about the most and circled them. Now, search your mind to see if you can think of anything else, even if it's not on your list #4, that the audience would find to be of high value, and add it to List #5.

If you have three to five items on your List #4 that have both a star to indicate their importance to you and a circle to designate them as important to your audience, these should be the main points for your speech. Sometimes you'll realize that an item from your audience's priorities on List #5 is so crucial to the listeners that it's worth making it a main point. There will also be occasions when you really do need to include an idea that is on your list that would never be on the listeners' list because they don't know they need it. You shouldn't ignore something that is central to their world, but don't dismiss your role as the expert who knows what's necessary. I pretty much force anyone who hires me to use "audience analysis" though most people aren't familiar with this phrase and therefore wouldn't ask for it. For me, and inevitably for them, audience analysis is the whole ball game. Blending the priorities of you as the speaker (List #4) and them as the audience (List #5), considering additions from your side or theirs should give you the best main points for the audience. This is the easiest way.

If you only have one or two items marked as important to both you and the audience, look again at List #5 and see if something marked as a priority for them should also be important to you. If there are no items that are important to both, you should revisit your topic to be certain that it's the best match for the audience and try to choose a couple of points from their list and one or two from your own that will go together well.

The number of main points will depend largely on your time limit. If you have 20 minutes or less, try to choose two to three main points. If you have 30 to 60 minutes, then you might have time for four or five points. You always want to have enough time to give at least some support — testimony, examples, statistics or an explanation for each main point. Based on your priorities and those of your audience, if you only had time to tell them two to five sentences, what would those be? Those are your main points. Although people like top-10 lists, it's hard for the audience to remember more than five key points, regardless of how much time you have. Even if you are conducting a four to eight hour training session, you shouldn't use more than five main categories of ideas for your audience to take away. Also, the word "main" starts to lose its value if you have too many points. It's like saying you have 10 favorite colors or 15 best friends. Sounds silly, doesn't it?

Next, decide on the order of the main points, again from the audience's perspective if possible. What would the listeners care most about hearing first? Sometimes, there is a logical flow to the order of points. If you're helping people learn a process, there might be a piece that must come before the others. You don't bake the cookies and then roll the dough. So, if there is a natural chronological order, go ahead and use it. Otherwise, often it is best to use a problem-solution format. Address one or more of their problems or challenges first so that they have reason to listen to the rest. Then describe the solution(s) to ease their pain and improve their results. When possible, start each main point with an active verb. Instead of "audience analysis," say "analyze your audience." This will help lead your audience to action and an understanding of what they can do when they leave your speech. It is virtually impossible to change their lives without getting them to act on something you've said.

As wonderful as action is, it can be good to at least consider using what I call your "vulnerability piece" as a main point. This can be especially effective when it is about your overcoming a challenge that your audience might also find to be a barrier to their own success.

<u>Strength in Vulnerability</u>!

We briefly touched on this in Chapter 4 in Karen's example, but it is worth examining further here. Whether you decide to use it as a main point or as an example to support one of your main points, you absolutely need to include something about your own vulnerability if possible. Usually, people try to avoid this. We think that we should show no weaknesses. We have to know all to be considered an expert in our field. And we certainly don't want people to see us as flawed because then they will not trust us as business professionals and will almost certainly not hire us. Please do yourself a favor and let go of this thinking.

No one knows everything. No one is perfect. Admitting weakness actually shows that you are aware enough to recognize it and strong enough to share it, which also indicates you're honest and willing to learn. Therefore, you'll be better at helping others, whatever your profession. Always remember the following:

Trust is reciprocal!

If you trust someone, chances are he or she will be much more likely to trust you. How do you actively trust an entire audience if you're the speaker? You tell them something personal, and share an example of your own that reveals a challenge, imperfection or learning experience of yours. Here's what the audience will think of this strategy:

• Because they'll tell the truth about something that's difficult for them, they'll probably tell the truth about other things.

• Because they are trust-ING, they are probably trust-WORTHY.

• Because they are strong enough to admit this, they must be very confident and good at what they do.

• Because they allowed themselves to learn from a challenge, they're more likely to be better at what they do than people who think they know it all and are closed off to improving.

• Because they can trust me (us) with that, then I can trust them with my business.

Here are two examples to show you what I mean:

At a luncheon for a chamber of commerce, I neglected to include my vulnerability piece. This was an audience (70 or so people) whom I did not know as well as in the following example, so I particularly needed to humble myself with that crowd in my 20-minute speech.

For the second example, I was speaking to a delightful group of ladies with whom I meet every month. This group is an independent business women's organization (Lunch Bunch, for short). This time, I had the pleasure of knowing my audience (of 20 or so) fairly well in advance of my 20-minute presentation. Here is how each speech went.

Chamber of Commerce:
Although the speech went well according to feedback from a few listeners, it felt a little off to me. I just didn't sense as deep a connection as I thought I should have made with this very friendly and honorable audience. Just before I spoke, I added some information to compliment two of the speakers who preceded me — one of whom was a high school student. This tactic is kind and establishes a common bond among audience members and between the audience and myself because we all listened to those speakers. It also was clearly not scripted or planned for, making it more spontaneous and sincere. However, I did not strike out anything from my notes to leave out, as I should have. What I ended up dropping due to time constraints was my vulnerability piece. I completely forgot to include it! I was talking about how to make a speech about the audience and I didn't help them trust me by trusting them. I had planned to tell them that when I get up to speak at networking events, there are times when I don't say quite what I wanted or I don't use my time as efficiently as I could or I break one of my own rules by not having a strong enough closing sentence.

The point would have been that perfection is <u>not</u> the goal. It's not always going to go just how we want it to go even when the presenter has been speaking for a long time and does it for a career. And that's not only normal, it's often good because audiences need to see speakers as human because that relieves the pressure on them. So, instead of more of the audience members giving stronger feedback and thinking all the previously listed bullets under trust being reciprocal, here's my guess as to their possible thoughts.

- *She doesn't make mistakes, so she couldn't help me with mine.*
- *She doesn't seem to be nervous, so she's nothing like me.*
- *She doesn't have much in common with me, so she wouldn't understand me.*
- *She doesn't relate to me, because I can't do what she's doing like she's doing it.*
- *She doesn't seem particularly open, so I would struggle to be open with her.*

Audience members will usually find speakers more appealing when the speakers let their guard down at least to some extent. Because I skipped this imperative part, the listeners did not feel that I had trusted them with anything significant. Although they took notes, laughed, appreciated the specific compliments to their organization and overall thought it was a good presentation, the presentation didn't generate the "wow" that I personally had wanted it to be because I didn't let them in on my humanity. Therefore, as outsiders to each other, we could only connect to a lesser degree. The listeners might not have consciously left thinking, "She didn't trust us" or "I don't trust her," but they were likely not as impressed as they would've been if I had helped them be even more comfortable.

Lunch Bunch:
In showing these women how to make their own presentations all about their audiences, I told them about this vulnerability piece and why it is so important. I ex-

plained how it works and how people respect a speaker more, not less, when the speaker shows a chink in her armor or drops the armor altogether. For my own example, I told them that personally my most difficult audiences are my own two sons who were at that time seven and four and one-half years old. I don't always know what they're trying to tell me, I often don't know how to explain something to them, I struggle with how to reach them, and I sometimes lack patience while doing all these things. I admitted that there are times I'd rather trade talents and not "get" adults as well, but be naturally better with my own kids. It seems that I have to work very hard at what other parents do so easily.

The results of this vulnerability were visibly obvious. The listeners looked more attentive, nodded with me, leaned toward me and clearly connected with me on a deeper level than they had before that point. One woman was teary and ended up sharing a story of her own with me after the speech. Another listener took my Leaders Speak program six months later. I referred to this "Lunch Bunch" example of sharing vulnerability and she said she remembered it vividly and that it was the most powerful part of my presentation and she would never forget it.

I had trusted the audience with very personal information and the listeners appreciated it and I could sense them trusting me back. I became someone more real for them, not just a speaker, but a person who is imperfect, frustrated at times and willing to talk about it in order to improve.

What happened because of allowing myself to be vulnerable is that everything else I said became more credible because I said something that many people would find hard to say. Sometimes we fear that we will be less credible or not taken as seriously if we admit something personal, especially in a professional setting, but the opposite is almost always true because trust is reciprocal. Some people allow their vulnerability to be entertaining for the audience. If you're not overly critical of yourself, an amusing, self-deprecating story can be a wonderful way to incorporate humor in a manner that is not offensive, but natural.

People love to laugh! Just be careful not to be too harsh with yourself because then the audience gets slightly uncomfortable and their laughter could be more nervous than enjoyable. Whether humorous or not, vulnerability will expedite your trust relationship with your audience. When we open that door to them, it will be open from their side as well.

When you're choosing main points, keep your vulnerability idea in mind. And if you don't use it as a whole category, you can still use it as evidence or a story example under another point. Once you have decided on those main ideas and are creating an outline or making your notes, include signposting on each main point. Words like "first", "second", "third", and "last" help your audience remember the same priorities you meant for them to recall. View them as mile markers on a trip that help your audience follow along with how far you've gone, how much you've got left to go, and which stops are most important to keep in mind. Save these words for the main points only and do not use them for smaller subpoints. If you have steps or transitions between other ideas, use the word "next" instead of signposts for those.

Choose two to five main points first, and keep your full list (#4) handy to decide next what ideas, examples, statistics, stories, or quotes you'll use to support those. Always consider your audience, their language, their priorities, and their perspective. Whether it is a main or supporting point, remember to include something that will make you vulnerable, yet related to the topic at hand. You don't want to be vulnerable with something completely off topic because that can look like you're just trying to gain favor. Trust them with something relevant so that the opportunity will be open for them to trust you.

Remember that each point you have called out as a main category must have some type of support. There are many ways to tell stories to illustrate your ideas.

ACTION ITEMS – Chapter 7:

• Write down your List #4 – Your Priorities, listing at least 10 items you could talk about on this topic, regardless of the audience, and then star your top three to five that are most important to you.

• Read over your List #2 – Your Audience, to remind yourself of their perspective. Circle the top three to five things from List #4 that are most important to your audience. Write those items down as your List #5 – Audience Priorities, and try to add at least one more thing that would be important to them on this topic and that wasn't even on your full List #4.

• Choose your two to five main points from the items on Lists #4 and #5 to be the things you want your audience to remember and use.

• Even if you have an aversion to outlines, make at least a rough one, using a signpost and an active verb at the start of each main point if possible (such as the earlier example of "analyze the audience" rather than "audience analysis") and leave room under each main point for the stories or pieces of information that will support them.

• Write down at least one relevant anecdote or example that you could share with your audience to make you somewhat vulnerable with your listeners.

LIST EXAMPLES

List #4 – Your Priorities

Client: Lisa, Founder and Chairwoman of the Board for Safe Place for Kids

Audience: Northland Chamber of Commerce

* = Top Three Most Important to the Speaker
◯ = Top Three Most Important to the Audience

- *Safe housing
- *For children
- *Build structures
- Kids in state custody, abused or neglected
- NOT run program
- NOT Habitat, but we're like it for kids
- Partner with organizations
- Orgs like Juvenile County, Counsel Center
- Program vs. corporation
- Give to community
- The building
- Give grant money
- Not "Safe Place" (at YMCA/QuikTrip)

List #5 – Audience Priorities

Client: Lisa, Safe Place for Kids

Audience: Northland Chamber of Commerce

◯ - Transfer circled words from List #4 as Important to the Audience

- For children
- Give to the community
- Give grant money

Add to Audience list:
- Kids in the same area as Chamber who are homeless
- Kids have to be sent to another city because not enough facilities here

RESULTING MAIN POINTS
(with active verbs to start wording) that both speaker and audience will relate to best and consider important:

1. Help children (from both speaker and audience priority lists)
2. Build buildings (from speaker priority list)
3. Give money (from audience priority list)

.

"There have been great societies that did not use the wheel, but there have been no societies that did not tell stories."

~ Ursula K. Le Guin, author

Chapter 8 – "Storytelling 101"

"This just happened earlier this week. A woman in our subdivision lives on my same street, in a similar house, with a similar family and really a similar life to mine. In one moment, her life was changed forever because she was in a car accident a few days ago. Sometimes fate throws a dart and it happened to hit her. It could have been me. It could have been any of us here. So, you see, at Aflac, it is not statistics that we are protecting. We are protecting real people with faces, families and lives like ours. We want to have shared what we do with everyone possible so that when tragedy strikes, we are already in place to help them through it."

At a State Kick-off Meeting, a client of mine, Jeremy, State Sales Coordinator for Aflac, told this true story to hundreds of his leaders, employees, and their spouses. He connected with his audience through their humanity. He connected his audience to their clients and potential clients through the common bond of awareness that accidents like this can and do happen to real people like them. He connected his audience to the importance of what they do, giving their careers deeper meaning. He inspired them by reminding them that they can do something about this. No other wording would have had the same effect that telling this story did. It was personal, timely and relevant. Jeremy impressed and motivated his people by relating this woman's story in a very powerful way.

Most of us have loved hearing stories since we were very young. It doesn't seem like work, and it doesn't seem fabricated when we learn information in a story. There are many ways to tell stories. We can tell them with numbers or statistics, pictures, or hands-on activities. We can tell others' stories like Jeremy did, share our own stories, or even give hypothetical examples. Whenever possible, the best stories are the real ones because they give your presentation credibility, sometimes heart and maybe even humor.

See if this sounds familiar. You listened to a speaker who was fairly dependent on her notes for the start of her presentation, the statistical evidence and some of the information. However, when she got to the story she was using as an example of her point, she looked up more, walked around a bit, gestured with her hands some, and generally seemed more comfortable. This is because she was talking to you instead of speaking at you. It felt less "speechy" to her and probably to you as well. This is very common. Sometimes it helps people to look at the entire presentation as a story to tell with some main stories (points) inside the larger whole. Always remember that you like hearing stories when you're in the audience. Doesn't it stand to reason that, when you're speaking, your audiences will also want to hear stories?

In this chapter, we'll discuss how many stories to use, story length, how to choose which stories to share, and how to use them to get your audience to visualize and connect your stories to their own.

How Much Storytelling to Do

A good rule of thumb is to give at least one example for each main point. When possible, these should be real, rather than hypothetical. Examples or stories give the audience a more specific picture in their minds of what you're explaining. This story might be told using a visual aid or with statistics, but you should view each main point as a chapter in the larger story. Pieces of information should connect, flow and lead into each other. You can always add transitions after you've written the body of a speech, but it's best if one part follows another naturally. On the other hand, you don't want to string a bunch of stories together and leave the audience entertained, yet wondering what the point was. If you've chosen main themes based on your specific audience, then you're on the right track and can use your stories to explain those topics.

Stories should not go on and on. Watch your time limit. Figure approximately an equal amount of time for each main point so that it's balanced. Even if you have plenty of time, you don't want to ramble. However, you should give enough details

so that the audience can envision what you're saying. The specifics are what make the story more real
for the listeners. You want them to be able to relate
to the character in the story and not just think of
them as someone in the life of the speaker who is
trying to make a point. If they think, "That happened to my sister" or "I've felt that way, myself,"
you've given an appropriate amount of detail for
them to visualize. Then, even if you think it's crystal
clear, go ahead and explicitly state why you've used
that story. Let the listeners know what point you're
making so that it isn't just a good story but provides
the lesson or tool that goes along with it. That's how
they'll be able to naturally learn and use what
you're explaining to them.

Choosing Which Stories to Tell
As always, consider your audience. If you're speaking to economists or financial advisers, you probably will want to use some statistics and build stories
around those. Basing the stories on numbers will
help the audience better relate to them because
you're using their language, which makes any story
more credible to them. However, don't just list a
batch of numbers without elaborating on the importance to your point. Use them to illustrate your
story. Clearly make the connection to your purpose.
Stringing together numbers by themselves doesn't
impress people nearly as much as telling the audience why you're bringing them up so they see how
the example fits into your bigger picture (or story).

If you are talking to a group of coaches of any kind — business, life, athletic, or musical, then you will probably fare better by using a story that is fairly personal, whether it's about yourself or another real person. Again, try to use a real, not a hypothetical, account if you can. Here is where we can examine some of the differences in support for your main points.

Although it seems like pigeonholing, most people lean toward either being thinkers or feelers. Thinkers are usually logic driven, analytical, want to hear facts, hard data, and possibly see graphs to compare or contrast results. Feelers are more likely to be emotion driven, empathetic, want to hear perspectives, instincts, and perhaps see a video example with strong characters. Within one type of group, you might have more of one kind of person or the other. Accountants will be more commonly thinkers, and coaches will be more probably feelers. However, if you only support your main points with stories surrounding logic, then you're likely to lose the connection with the feelers. On the other hand, if you solely use emotional appeals, then you'll be missing the boat with any thinkers in your audience. The key is to mix it up to cover all your bases, but still have the majority of your support match the majority of your audience type.

When you can tell success stories, those show your audience how something has really worked and often why. If possible, choose examples that are relevant to the people in your audience. For instance, if you are speaking to realtors and don't have a realtor example, pick a story about a mort-gage broker, which is closer to their world than say, a welder. If you're talking to mechanics, then you might do better to use the welder example. If you have a group of people who know each other and have an example of a person whom you've helped who is actually in that audience and you know there will not be any confidentiality concerns, then use the example with that individual. The fact that you helped someone the rest of the audience knows in-herently has more credibility in their minds and re-inforces the common bond among them and be-tween you and them. The more specific your story is, the more specific the audience's connection will be to it and to you because it helps them picture that image. It also assists them in relating to you and to those you've already served, which makes them more likely to hire you to also help them.

My client Kathleen (from Chapter 2) was prepar-ing to present to a utility company. One of the things she talks about is the fact that we think in pictures. When we hear the word apple, we do not picture in our minds the letters in a row a-p-p-l-e, instead we envision an actual apple. For the utility company, I asked her if we could change her own example. Rather than use an apple, which doesn't have anything particularly to do with her audience, we used something from their world. I sug-gested we use one of their pictures − an outlet. She used that and said that we do not picture the letters o-u-t-l-e-t, instead we picture a real outlet. We even took it a step further to say that while a layperson might imagine the outside of an outlet that we see on a wall, they (as professionals in the business) might see the wires beneath the cover. Again, this feels less "canned" to an audience because the listeners know you wouldn't say exactly the same thing to a different group of people who don't work at a utility company. This is the kind of tactic that gives them the sense that it was all about them and that you paid them a great gesture of respect. Look how easy a change that was for Kathleen to make. A small amount of time can often yield a big payoff in reception from the audience!

If most people in your audience are in a visual field such as landscaping, interior design or graphic arts, chances are that they are primarily visual learners. This means they'll appreciate visual aids to enhance what you're saying. Many people like to see visual aids, but this is especially true of people who are visual themselves. Just remember to use the visual aid to tell your story. Don't make a chart that just repeats facts or numbers you've already stated. Use ideas that will help your audience grasp what you're saying. For example, don't just say that some number of tons of garbage has been collecting in our landfills. Give a comparison such as "this is enough to fill twenty giant 747 jets." That we can picture. Often you can find these comparisons online where you got the original statistics. It helps people to picture the vastness of what you're saying, making it more concrete instead of abstract and hard to truly comprehend. We'll talk more about how to use visual aids later, but for now, just keep in mind that they can help you tell your story. However, a visual aid by itself is not enough without the story to go with it, so it shouldn't look like you just threw together a visual aid because you knew you were supposed to include one.

Get the Audience to Connect Your Stories to Theirs
We've talked about mentioning a common ground you have with your audience, using the group's language, and adapting to them with relevant examples and support. These things will all aid you in getting the listeners to see how your stories can have an impact on their stories.

Giving specifics is one way to help your audience visualize what you're saying. Think of it as actually painting a picture for them. A picture of two people with a blue background doesn't necessarily inspire us. However, if someone describes for us the expressions on the individuals' faces that suggest certain emotions, the positions in which the people are sitting that reveals their comfort level, or the different shades of blue that indicate the time of day and weather, then we begin to really view the scene in our minds, even without seeing it with our own eyes. This kind of explanation causes your audience members to visualize what you're saying, thereby engaging the minds of your listeners. Once the people can really picture it themselves, their minds will next fill in what they can relate to in the picture. Have they experienced something similar themselves? Have they heard a story like this from someone close to them? Better yet, can they imagine this same type of thing happening to them in the future? Going back to the story Jeremy told at the Aflac meeting, part of why it had such influence on his audience was because they could imagine that incident happening to them or their loved ones.

This is your real key. If you can get people to visualize themselves in your story, example and lesson, that is when your points will really sink in deeply. If they are connecting your story or stories with the potential stories that they want for themselves, then they will be motivated to spend more time with you, listen to you again, and even hire you. If they picture the kind of success that everyone needs help reaching because there is so much power in both an outside perspective and holding each other accountable, then you are becoming part of their journey. If you connect with individuals in your audience in a way that causes them to picture you assisting them on their paths to further accomplishments, then you have already begun building relationships that can be springboards to crucial alliances down the road.

This collaborative approach is important to recognize in your own business and imperative for you to impress upon your audiences. You have the ability to act on your own, but sharing your goals with others and utilizing each other's talents to supplement strengths is a formula for greater reach and impact. You have an opportunity every time you speak to a group to illustrate for all your listeners how much more they can do, how much better they can be, and how much further they can go with you. When you get them to picture that next level or three levels past it, chances are they'll see that they can attain those goals quicker and easier with your help. Then, doors will begin to open for you and for them to help each other be mutually successful. Public speaking shouldn't just be for the moment. Remember that you're starting relationships full of future stories that can change lives!

Along with your stories related to your audience, another great way to reach people is to use words they will understand. Although you never want to script your entire speech because it becomes too stilted and less sincere, it is important to consciously craft some of your language so that you are artfully phrasing your words especially to reach your particular audience.

ACTION ITEMS – Chapter 8:

•   Review List #2 - Your Audience, and write down the names of at least three people with whom you've worked in your audience's field. Or, if you have worked with no one in that field, then name people you've worked with who are from closely related fields.

•   Write down how you helped those people overcome a challenge, discover a new idea or get a positive result.

- Incorporate a brief story or testimonial using an example from the previous Action Item or something similar for each main point, including visual aids or statistics if available.

"If you can't explain it simply, you don't understand it well enough."

~ Albert Einstein

Chapter 9 – Language is Powerful

A speaker says that the problem with the crankshaft was that there was an intake valve issue; or it was a cardiac infarction caused by chronic hypertension; or by the writ of habeas corpus, the precedent dictates this outcome; or due to insufficient RAM or inconsistent QA, the integrity of the data is compromised. If you've ever been in an audience and heard these types of phrases and didn't understand the concepts, it is not your lacking, it is the speaker's. Whether you're speaking to one person or a large group, it is your responsibility to speak to the audience's level. If you aren't sure what that is, you need to ask or else err on the side of very basic knowledge. You should incorporate wording and language from the audience's world as much as you can to include them and connect with them.

Back to the Basics
We often do not realize how much industry-specific jargon we use that others won't recognize. Have you ever heard anyone from medical, computer, legal, or mechanical fields use terms or acronyms

with which you were not familiar? We can all do this, but highly technical fields are particularly challenging. You should assume a variety of levels of knowledge including vocabulary words, acronyms, and abbreviations exist in every audience. Always assume you'll have lay people who won't know what you mean. Therefore, you should either avoid this type of jargon, or if you must use it, explain it at the most basic possible level.

You might be wondering whether you'll lose the people who are already familiar with the detailed aspects of the subject. Will they be bored or find your wording to be condescending? Certainly, you can word explanations by suggesting, "Some of you might know this, but in case not ..." You can ask your audience if they are familiar with a particular term or concept. The risk here is that some won't admit that they don't know. Also, if most raise their hands, then the others can feel particularly inadequate as though they should know. You don't want to embarrass your audience members. You can tell them that you didn't used to know the answer until someone explained it to you, which shows your own vulnerability.

Overall, you need to assume that those who know your world and terms already have a higher level of interest along with their higher level of knowledge so they'll continue listening and be more comfortable than those for whom it's quite new. Be willing to use the audience if it's a mix and if you have time. Ask your seasoned veterans on the topic how they would explain something. When everyone hears a few different ways to explain the same thing, your chances increase that one description will connect with each "green" listener. Also, you'll make a more positive impression when you share the floor with your audience, so that you're not the only one who gets to talk, who has valuable information, or who can help others comprehend. Most importantly, if you speak above the heads of some of your audience, they will at least not be able to take away with them the value that they would have otherwise, and at worst they will leave with a negative sense of self, you, the topic, or the entire event.

A colleague of mine, Steve, facilitates a region of Business Network International (BNI) and teaches his members to break their businesses down to the most basic parts when they stand up to describe them for the group. Don't assume that "everyone knows that." Often they don't! He suggests that they pretend they're talking to third graders. This is not an insult to the audience, it is an aid. If you can explain your business to a third grader in a way in which he can comprehend it, then you'll have almost certainly either avoided confusing jargon or explained it at such a basic level that the elementary student would be able to follow and understand. If a third grader can understand it, then we as adults can not only comprehend it ourselves, but also will have an easier time in sharing the information with others.

In any group presentation, imagine an audience member (named Susan) gets asked by someone who couldn't make it (Jan), "What did the speaker say?" Susan will likely give a general gist of the overall topic. What if Susan could instead explain the main ideas and include a specific example that would illustrate how Jan could utilize your information, products, or services. Without necessarily realizing it, you taught Susan to sell for you, and Jan might become one of your best clients even though she didn't attend. It would be because you connected the information so strongly for Susan that she was able to relate, remember, and repeat it to another! Making it repeatable is how you can create spokespeople in every audience.

To facilitate this type of connection and spreading result, you will also want to incorporate words from your audience's world when possible. If they say "clients," then so should you. If they use the word "customers," then that's what you'll want to say. Find out what some of their jargon is so that if it's not too complicated, and you know you can refer to it correctly, then you can use that as well.

Speak in the Audience's Language

You wouldn't give a speech to a Spanish audience in English or vice versa. Make sure that you use as much of your audience's common language as possible. Also, don't use too much of your own jargon if it's unfamiliar to the listeners. Whenever you are going to speak to a group or meet with potential clients or new customers, check out their company so you get a sense of their culture. Check out the company's website to look particularly at its values, mission, goals or vision, (under "About" or "Info") and, of course, the home page. Usually the company's priorities, those things are most important to them, will show up in these places. Speakers don't always realize that anything the company leaders have put on their home page is important to them. If there is a press release section, review some of the recent ones to see what activities they are proud of such as leadership changes or new locations. Some people don't do this website check. They think it will take a lot of time, or don't think this research will matter. Other people only focus on the sales descriptions such as what the organization offers in products or services. However, this is not sufficient information because other companies probably sell the same things they sell. You need to see what is unique about a particular company. Still other people know they're supposed to consider the audience's background, but they don't necessarily understand how to incorporate what they find. Knowing how to use the information will help determine what you should take away from your research.

The American Business Women's Association (ABWA) hired me to do a presentation on "Negotiating in Business and in Life." In order to know what they might want to hear about that topic and how they might use that information, I needed to find out what the group was. I needed to know who they were, what the members valued, what I had in common with them and what results they wanted. The easy answer with no work at all, just common sense, was that they are women in business who value getting together and want to negotiate better. I have all those traits in common with them. However, this barely scratched the surface. I needed to go deeper to really understand my audience and learn their language. Why would someone join ABWA instead of another group? What is appealing and what is special about them? Here's what I found on their websites.

National site:
- *Home page:*
    - *Leadership*
    - *Education*
    - *Networking support*
    - *Recognition*

- *Mission:*
    - *Bring together*
    - *Provide opportunities*
    - *Grow personally and professionally*

Chapter site:
- *Home page:*
    - *Professional development*
    - *Networking support*
    - *Recognition*
    - *Exact mission statement from the national site*

- *History:*
    - *Education and training remain the cornerstone*
    - *Had name change a few months before my speech*

Notice that the chapter I would be speaking to called out a couple of the terms from the national site and used the wording "professional development" in addition to "education." That told me which of the national site's priorities were most important to this particular chapter.

Therefore, when speaking to them, I mentioned their focus on bringing people together in "negotiating," not looking at it as a one versus the other mentality, but as a joint effort. I discussed the focus they have on education as evidence that they are willing to learn and suggested that they be willing to learn in negotiating. Learn what is important to the other person.

They also had been through a chapter name change, and I referenced that, pointing out that they probably had to negotiate with each other when going through the decision-making process.

Again, as in the earlier example from Chapter 3, the listeners' physical reactions were noticeable. When they heard their own mission not just mentioned in passing, but connected to the content topic of the presentation, they nodded their heads, leaned forward, and seemed more engaged. They realized that this information was especially for them, not intended for every audience. They connected more deeply with the strategies they could take away to use and with me as a speaker who respected them enough to help them make that valuable connection, which would in turn bring them increased results in their own businesses and lives.

Let's remember that all these concepts work outside of public speaking, in every communication interaction. Where is the other person coming from, what is his or her perspective? Why might we not be on the same page at times? How can I reach them? The following example shows that business group audiences are not the only ones who benefit from this careful wording. An individual, personal audience of one can be affected in a similar way.

A former student was taking my Interpersonal Communication class and preparing for our relationship change project. She chose her 8-year-old stepson as the person with whom she wanted to improve her communication. She was concerned that she wanted to be true to herself and not try to be someone she's not, yet sincerely wanted to do better communicating with him. She was frustrated that he would not tell her the whole story at times when something hadn't gone exactly according to plan. She sensed that he was nervous around her and recognized that she is a very direct person and might be intimidating to him.

We discussed small ways she could change her side of their interactions without being too different from her natural self. She decided she could first ask him questions that were not "loaded" (assuming he had done something wrong), use a softer tone, and choose slightly different wording in her reactions to his answers that might seem less attacking. She would be just a little less abrupt, tell him that she appreciated his willingness to talk to her, and give him some indication that she really wants to understand his perspective — why something occurred or what his opinion of it was. These small wording changes in how she phrased her questions, responses and appreciation made a huge difference and her stepson almost immediately changed his communication with her as a result. He was more open, talkative, and straightforward with her because he (at some level, at least) realized that she was trying to help him and meet him in the middle instead of only asserting her parental authority.

Her changes were minor, yet over a couple of months, they made a big impact. After the class and semester were over, she confided in me that she and her husband had been planning not to have any more children. This was mostly due to her feeling that she wasn't a very good mother to her stepson and therefore would not be a good mom to another child, either. Her ability to change her communication with her stepson resulted in their whole relationship being changed, and they ended up being closer. With this revelation, she became aware of the power she had to choose to be a better communicator and she and her husband decided to try to have another child together!

Does this wordsmithing seem petty? Would a little word difference here or there really matter? Do yourself the favor of trying it a few times with your own audiences of one or many and watch the difference in your immediate reception and your eventual results. After the aforementioned speech to the ABWA, over the next six months, I received invitations to speak to two more groups based on recommendations from that original audience. And it was life changing for my student to improve her relationship with her stepson. How's that for powerful?

ACTION ITEMS – Chapter 9:

•   Review your List #2 - Your Audience to see if any phrasing or terms occur to you that they would all use regularly.

•   Even if you already visited the company's website when creating one of your earlier lists, go back to it now and pay particular attention to the wording, especially in those four critical areas: home page, values, mission, and goals or vision.

•   Ask the gatekeeper who scheduled you to speak what some important words from the audience's world would be.

•   Incorporate in your actual notes some of their language, preferably one term or phrase they use often for each of your main points.

"What we call the beginning is often the end. And to make an end is to make a beginning. The end is where we start from."

~ T. S. Eliot, poet

Chapter 10 – Start Strong and Finish Strong!

We've all heard that you don't get a second chance to make a first impression. And first impressions can be long lasting and difficult to shake. The first line of your speech is your first impression as a speaker. In fact, the entire introduction is key to getting the audience interested enough to listen to the rest of your presentation. Ask yourself why they should care about anything you're about to say and answer that in your introduction. Just as I've stressed throughout this book, the introduction should be all about the audience!

Besides the start being crucial, the end is also important. Your conclusion is what you leave the audience with right before they exit the room. Although you don't usually hear the phrase, you could think of it as your "last impression" as a speaker until you meet again, if ever. So don't dismiss the conclusion of your speech as unimportant. You don't want to be right on the mark for most of your presentation and then minimize that effect with a weak ending.

The first part of this chapter will cover the three most critical pieces of your introduction in the order in which you should present them: your attention-getter (first line), your credibility, and your preview sentence. The second part will address the two components of your conclusion: your review sentence and your memorable closing line.

And Now, Introducing...

<u>You Never Get a Second Chance to Start Your Speech</u>
Notice that although this is the first comment you make, I'm addressing it in the tenth chapter of this book. That is no accident. Earlier, we discussed that the hardest part of making an effective speech can be getting started. This is what happens when you try to start at the beginning. It sounds like it would make sense, but this is not the best way to proceed. Much audience analysis needs to be done before you write any content. Even with the actual information for the speech, you should start by choosing your main points, then your support or stories and then your introduction because before that you don't know yet what you are introducing.

The two most common ways I hear people start presentations are: "I'm Jody Cross" or "Thank you (for coming or for the introduction someone else just said about you)." Neither of these is exciting and neither builds toward your topic. These are not attention-grabbing statements. Who cares what the speaker's name is? Unless you're famous, your name is not exciting. If you are really famous, then you probably don't need to tell the audience your name at all because it's something they already know. People tend to feel that it's polite to introduce yourself and thank the audience for coming, and it would be rude not to thank someone who just introduced you. There are more important things than being polite. And if you must, you can be polite with a little different timing yet not waste your first impression on something cliché (or at least common) and not focused on the whole audience.

There is an idea called "primacy theory," which says that we remember the first thing we heard. This makes the opening line very important. Stating your name or thanking the audience for coming aren't the end of the world, but if you use these, you would be missing an opportunity to capitalize on that natural impact that the first line has. Take that chance to truly get the attention of the audience because you've piqued their curiosity, caused them to visualize something, or made them look forward to what you'll say next.

Another thing that speakers often do is deviate from their plan. They carefully choose a first line that would naturally gain the audience's attention and lead into their topic. Then, they get front and center on stage and say something else first! If you say, "hello," "thank you," "please take your seats," "there's water and coffee at the back," or "before we get started…" then you have just started. Your first line was whatever sentence you literally spoke first.

This means that when you say the line you actually planned to be your opening, it will not have the impact that it could have because it wasn't the first thing said. Filler sounds like "um" or "OK" also reduce this impact. Anything that you say or the audience hears from your mouth before the attention getter you planned will take away from that line's impact.

If you need to do any housekeeping (talk about the location of bathrooms, coffee, etc.) do it after your attention-getter and not as your very first line. Here are some things you do want to do with your first line. Make your opening about the audience. This sets an other-oriented tone for the whole presentation that is not accomplished by "my name is ..." You can do this by asking the audience a question. When you ask them a question, everyone answers it in their head, even if they don't raise their hand or shout out a comment. This means that you have engaged the minds of your audience when you ask them something because humans naturally think of their answer. Make it clear whether you want hands raised, answers given, or are posing a rhetorical question for them to consider silently. Also, give them time to answer if you want responses. If you mean a line to be rhetorical and they think you want an answer or hands raised, they can be embarrassed and you don't want that. You don't want to do anything that makes your listeners uncomfortable. If it's meant to be rhetorical, you could change the wording to "Imagine this ..." or "Think about this ..." If you have time to hear some responses, an open-ended question is beneficial because it immediately gets the audience involved. You can do an icebreaker that allows the crowd to get to know each other a bit, but don't have it be too long, and make sure it's clear why they're doing it. Often, this exercise would be better placed in one of the main points once the listeners know a little about what to expect from you and from the entire presentation. Humor also can be used as long as it leads into your topic and is not disjointed from what comes next, which can leave your audience confused.

You can establish a common bond between the audience and yourself or compliment the audience. These two strategies only work if you can be specific enough that they see that you're sincere. General commonalities or praise only seem like you're trying to gain favor without much to back up your statement. You can tell a story that is about someone with a background similar to their own, or at least the problem or challenge is similar to one they regularly face. Set a scene for the listeners, taking them to another place or time. One of the most famous first lines ever was President Abraham Lincoln's Gettysburg Address. "Four score and seven years ago ..." is mainly what you remember. That kind of wording immediately captures your attention because it takes you away from your current time and circumstance. It is as if you have travelled elsewhere with the speaker. You can use a startling statistic or a quote as long as you can explain why that is important to the listeners and it leads into your topic. You can use a visual or sensory aid — again if you connect it clearly to the audience and your point. The primary underlying message of your first sentence will almost always be one of two choices. Either it will convey, "This is about me, the speaker" or "This is about you, the audience." The latter concept will immediately form a stronger connection with the listeners and make them more interested in everything else you want to say, and make them more likely to hire, support or believe you as a result of your speech. It is worth making the most of this opportunity. It is the simplest change you can make to your speeches that will have a dramatic effect on your results.

Working in a corporate job, I once attended a community event at which a panel of five superintendents of large area school districts was speaking. The audience of hundreds was comprised primarily of teachers and classified staff from those districts, and also included other administrators, probably some parents and some friends of education like myself. Every single one of those five superintendents started by saying, "I'm so and so, superintendent of the such and such school district." That was all the time and attention they got. As one of them wrapped up, the audience members quieted to listen to what the next person would say. They listened intently for exactly one sentence and then turned to each other and started whispering to their neighbors again. This was happening all over the room. I could look around and see everywhere that most people were not engaged at all. Although this might sound irresponsible or even rude on the part of the audience, I believe it to be simply human nature. It is the speaker's responsibility to get the audience's attention and help them connect to the content. Many audiences have no more patience than that. If you do not grab them right away, you might have lost them for the duration. What a waste of everyone's time and energy.

Why Should We Listen to You?

Establishing your credibility is one of the trickiest parts of your presentation. You have to have something here. If you need brain surgery, you probably want to know that the surgeon is experienced and you wouldn't want a first year med student operating on you. You do need to tell the audience why you know more than the average person about your topic. However, you do not want to detail your entire resume, which isn't necessary, and would probably bore or even put off the listeners. Ask yourself why your resume items matter to your audience. It's not that the audience only wants to listen to someone with many years of experience just because they have those years. What is important is that listeners assume you have learned things that they don't already know because they don't have all those years of experience under their belts. Tell the audience what you've gleaned in all those years that could help them. Let them know what you gained from all your extensive education that could help them. Explain what the difference is be-

tween people with and people without your certifi-
cations that could help them get the results they
want to achieve.

See, you can make even your own credibility
be about your audience if you frame it correctly and
use words that help the audience learn from your
experience, your training, or even your mistakes.
The credibility also doesn't have to be extensive; too
many details about your background can appear
egotistical. Also, don't discuss too much about your
past. Unless there is a "variety is the spice of life"
angle or one seemingly unrelated job helped you
see another perspective in your current job, then
your audience won't care that you have had several
careers. Again, ask yourself why they should care. If
it's just a matter of wanting them to know you better so that they feel more comfortable and trust you
more, then you can pepper that throughout the rest
of the speech. Just don't go into too much detail
about you. Remember, the tone you want to set is
that it is about the audience.

Many people, including authors of public
speaking textbooks, suggest that you include other
angles in your introduction such as stating your
purpose, explaining the importance of the topic, and
establishing a common ground with your audience.
These points are valid but they can often be done
along with one of the three crucial pieces: the attention getter, the credibility and the preview. Generally, a brief introduction is better than a long one, so
you don't want to go on forever to the point at
which the audience wonders when you'll get into

the main course. The last thing you do need is the preview.

A Sign of Things to Come

The preview of main points helps your audience know what to expect. Remember that we have discussed that expectations have a great deal to do with how satisfied we are with something. If you give a clear preview, it's much less likely that any member of your audience will get to the end of your presentation and think, "That's not what I thought this speech was going to be." Your preview acts as a road map to let your audience know where you're taking them. Often, particularly creative people will sense that the preview seems redundant or otherwise interrupts the flow. However, if it's done smoothly, it can provide a nice transition into the body of your speech. Even if not done superbly, it is more important to have it than to have a flawless flow. It helps people know what to listen for and remember later. As I've already explained, everyone has a different frame of reference, so the clearer you are about the main ideas you want your audience to remember above all else, the more likely they are to recall what you marked as most important. If they are taking notes, it can also help them to organize their notes in a way that will help them recall which stories or examples are meant to illustrate which points.

Your preview of main points is one of the easiest things to add if you've written your main points in the body clearly. Keep in mind that if you make the wording of your main points concise, they are easier to preview, easier to catch, and easier to remember for your audience. Also remember that if you have started each with an active verb, then you are already leading your audience throughout your whole speech toward the actions you want them to take when they leave. For the preview, you simply tell them how many points to expect and list them in the same order with exactly the same wording. Here's an example. "We're going to look at three ways our expansion can help you, our customers: secure more locations, offer more jobs, and provide more services." It's that easy. Do not try to give each main point a longer explanation. Keep it simple and brief. Include it as the very last sentence in your introduction, just before you go into the body or bulk of the first point. This will set the stage for your audience to remember your main ideas and probably even be able to relay them to someone who missed your speech.

   If you are introduced by someone else or you have a sponsor(s) for the event, you can thank that person, people or company at the appropriate spot, as shown in the example that follows. If they read a bio, you can still make a brief credibility statement, but don't belabor the point when someone else has already made it. It's even more credible when you're not making the statement as long as the person introducing you is a good speaker, so opt for someone to introduce when you have a choice. If someone doesn't introduce you, you want to politely thank your sponsor, and you need the audience to know something practical, then here's a good approach.

How many of you consider public speaking to be something that leaders do? Excellent, everyone agrees. Well, I'm Jody Cross with Leaders Speak and in more than 20 years of public speaking, I've learned that people usually do see leaders speaking, so when they see someone who is speaking in public, they assume that person is a leader. Leaders Speak. Because you're all business owners, you probably wear many hats and "spokesperson" should be one of them so that you're seen as a leader in your field. Speaking of leaders, thank you, Val, for that kind introduction and thanks to Continental Title for being our event sponsor today and for always investing in educating our community. There are beverages at the back for you and restrooms just out the back to the right. We're going to have an interactive session today, so please ask questions or give input anytime. We're going to talk today about three ways that speaking publicly will help your business: increase credibility, increase clients and increase revenue.

Notice that the thank you and housekeeping lines were somewhere in the middle, not the first line where the attention-getter should always be, nor the last piece of the introduction, which should always be your preview. I'm going to go ahead and suggest that you:

Never thank the audience for coming!

I'm aware that many people will meet this idea with extreme resistance. However, just as I'm going to ask you to do with your audiences, I want to push you all a little out of your comfort zones to focus on what really matters. Actions speak louder than words. If you really want to thank your audience, do the Action Items in this book to truly make your presentation tailored specifically for them. Give them fantastic information, compelling reasons that your information is crucial, and clear explanations for how to use your ideas in their own work or lives. I've thanked many an audience for coming. So has everyone else. I've come to believe that it's probably more a waste of their time than beneficial to thank them for it. Anything we say just because everyone else does is probably not that meaningful and therefore needs to be reconsidered. I've decided to stop doing it myself and have started to advise all my audiences and clients to do the same. Furthermore, if people stay in the habit of saying it at all, they're more likely to say it as their first or last line where it doesn't belong. They would then be abandoning the opportunity to have a much stronger impact with that first or last impression.

It's a Wrap!

Just like there is a primacy theory that indicates the importance of the first line, there is also an idea called "recency theory" that says we remember the last thing we hear. There are usually only two pieces needed in the conclusion: the review and the memorable closing.

Review

Some people suggest that you signal the conclusion of a speech by actually saying, "In conclusion …" Some people do not agree. I'm not sure it's a big deal either way. It probably does sound a little speechy to say it, and I believe that a clear review can serve that purpose. If you start repeating the main points, the audience will usually realize that you're wrapping up your presentation. The review should sound exactly like the preview, except in past tense. Remind your listeners how many points to remember, list them in order and in the same wording you used in the preview and the body. Yes, it is repetitive. It is meant to be. It helps your audience remember the main points you want them to remember instead of the different tangents they heard through their frames of reference during the speech. The review should always be the first thing in the conclusion.

Closing Line

If you have housekeeping items to convey, such as where to go next or whether or not you'll be available for questions, or if you absolutely insist on saying the ever-popular, "Thank you for coming," do it after the review, but before your last line. You don't want to waste the natural impact your last line carries by just saying thank you. I still maintain that it's a formality that is so overused that it has become less sincere, so I say avoid it here just like you should in the introduction. Many people want to ask if there are any questions as their ending line, but that often provides an indistinguishable ending. Is it over after two questions, or 10 or 15 minutes' worth of questions, or does it go on indefinitely? Especially if there is a time limit, it's usually best to tell them that you will be around for those who have questions after the speech and then state your closing line. That way you aren't holding the rest of the individuals who have no questions hostage.

Believe it or not, people will actually say, "That's it." This is anticlimactic and makes you sound unorganized, as if you didn't really know how you were going to end the presentation and that you have no plan. Even if only subconsciously, this can indicate to your audience that there could be other times you don't have a plan when it seems like you probably should.

Another method that some people suggest is ending with a tag line that you want the listeners to remember. This is rarely a good choice. Unless you already have a very recognizable tag line, such as Nike – Just Do It, or an incredibly poignant line that concisely explains why people should hire you instead of a competitor, then it isn't likely to be very valuable to your audience. Tag lines are usually related to branding — something that is part of your brand image that you want people to associate with you when they hear or see it. Although these lines certainly have their place, it's usually not in the closing of your speech. Using them also brings the focus back to you or your organization instead of keeping it on the audience and what you want them to take away with them when they leave. What are they supposed to do when they hear your tag line? If that question isn't answered easily, then using a tag line is probably not your best ending.

What you can use to make the most of the natural impact for your memorable closing line is some kind of call to action. One of the best I've ever heard was by a client of mine, Nancy, who was speaking about cancer to a women's group. Within her presentation, she told her audience how her own story had progressed not once but twice to a diagnosis of and battle with cancer, both of those starting with a mammogram. After reviewing what she most wanted her audience to remember, she closed with this. "Please get your yearly mammogram. It saved my life — twice." There was not a dry eye in the room. She connected her story of survival to the desire that those women have to preserve their own health and possibly to their loved ones whom they've lost or who have also survived. Her last line combined a personal touch with a very easy, practical, important call to action that drove home her message.

When using a call to action, it can be fairly direct if you sense the audience will accept that. If you get the feeling that the audience will be turned off, you can soften the directness some so it doesn't sound like a sales pitch. Very direct could be something like, "Do not delay, call me today for a quote." Less direct could be, "If you want to learn more, contact me anytime." Either line or anything in between, depending on the audience, can work. If you are unsure what they'll be comfortable with, err on the side of less direct. You can also close with a startling statistic, quote, or story, but I'm a big believer in expecting something of your audience, so ideally, the stat or quote should at least imply action on the part of the audience. Other than the closing line, there generally shouldn't be any new information in your conclusion and it isn't meant to be very long.

One last strategy that can be effective is to somehow tie in your closing line to your opening line. For instance, in helping a roofer client, John, write his speech, we started it with this. "How many of you get your roof checked once a year?" We figured most people would probably not be able to raise their hands for this. Then we ended it with this. "Next time I ask, I hope all of you will be able to say that you do get your roof checked annually!" When your last line refers back to your first line, it provides a nice full circle feel for your audience, like you've come back around to close the loop that makes a neat package.

Challenging audiences can change lives!

One reason to do all of the connecting we've been talking about is so your listeners will allow you to help them in some way. Once you have established that you understand their world, made connections to them with stories, and provided great, active, main points they can use, then you can challenge them to act on all that. When you are in sync with your audience, that's when you can push them past the status quo to do something different. Be willing to extend that challenge, which will in turn extend your impact on them.

Just as I said not to make unnecessary sounds before your first line, don't be tempted to add something after you've spoken your last line. Let it hang there and have its desired effect. Remember that any housekeeping goes before your memorable closing. Don't add "Thank you" or "That's it" or anything else. If you've delivered your last line effectively, it should be clear you're ending. Even if it's not, just start heading back to your seat or off stage to one side and the listeners will get it and probably start applauding. Think of it this way, if you're really going to influence people's lives, then the very last thing they should hear you say is something they can do to begin that change.

Remember that your introduction and conclusion frame your body (your main story). An unframed picture is usually not nearly as impressive because it does not seem finished. Use your start and ending to create a positive first, last and lasting impression on your audience.

ACTION ITEMS – Chapter 10:

• Write down at least three ideas that could be your opening line. Think about which the audience would be most interested in and pick one.

• Write down at least three ideas that could be your credibility sentence. Ask yourself which the audience would care about the most and from which they could learn something and pick one.

• Write down your preview statement (preferably on your outline).

• Write down your review statement (preferably on your outline).

• Write down at least three ideas that could be your closing line. Think about which the audience would be most likely to do and pick one.

PART THREE:

Deliver for Your Audience

Chapters 11–15

"Words mean more than what is set down on paper. It takes the human voice to infuse them with deeper meaning."

~ Maya Angelou, author

Chapter 11 – That Sounds Good

People have given one of their most precious resources, their time, to hear you speak. Your audience will struggle to receive your content message if they have to work hard at overcoming distractions such as barely being able to hear or keep up with you. The volume, rate, fluidity and variety you use with your voice will determine whether or not your speech is effective and whether or not your listeners will get your point and their results.

<u>Say What?</u>
If there is no public address system and you're relying solely on your own volume, you simply must be loud enough for the very back of the room to hear you easily and clearly. Otherwise, what's the point of speaking at all?

Some people are naturally soft spoken, some get softer when they're nervous and some do both. If this is one of your tendencies, you need to practice yourself right out of that habit and into being your own megaphone. If you're this type of person, you will need to feel in your head as though you're yelling, at least until you become accustomed to a louder base volume. If you do not, chances are the back half of the audience (at least) will be frustrated with straining to try to hear you. They also might merely give up and start talking to each other, in which case, you are being too soft and getting competition for the audience's attention.

If possible, practice your speech to at least one person and have him sit at the back of the room you'll present in or a room that is similar in size. Don't just reach them with your voice; be louder than they even want. This shows you that you can be loud without being angry. It will begin to stretch your comfort zone to widen little by little, which will work for you with many challenging habits. If you do this often, you'll eventually be able to alter your speaking voice to a point at which you finally feel truly comfortable being louder. A client of mine who is a sales rep for a nationally recognized ice cream brand is one of those naturally soft-spoken people. We had her practice giving a speech to me, and each time I would move back so she had to project her voice more and more to reach me. Sure enough, when she focused on it, she was able to do it! When you are doing your actual presentation, be conscious of reaching the people in the back row. Watch them. If you see them leaning forward, tilting their head to the side and toward you or obviously putting their hand by their ear, then clearly you need to speak up for them. Otherwise, you are wasting their time.

Using a Microphone

Sometimes, even when a soft-spoken person has a microphone, if she doesn't hold it correctly, she can't be heard. Audience members will often ask for the volume of the system to be turned up, but the real problem may be with placement of the microphone in relation to the speaker's mouth. Be willing to test this in advance until you get it right for the back of the room. If it works fine during testing, then seems to be not working during the speech, take time to figure it out so that everyone will be able to hear you clearly. It is worth interrupting the flow of content to prevent your audience from feeling frustrated and missing part or all of what you're saying. Get the volume issues out of the way quickly so that everyone can focus on the message at hand.

If there is a microphone and it is working, then use it. Some people feel they are loud enough without one and feel it's more personal not to use one. They call out to the back of the room asking if they can be heard and get confirmation that they're fine. But a couple minutes in, they've dropped to a more comfortable, natural volume and their voice isn't reaching the back anymore. Also, listeners with hearing aids or other impairments might struggle but not want to admit it. So, if the microphone is an option, take it!

Personally, I've never heard anyone speak too loudly for their audience when only using their own vocal chords. However, even when there is a microphone available, other problems can arise if a speaker suddenly turns her head toward the micro-phone or moves it to be right in front of her mouth or gets too close to other equipment that creates that awful feedback sound. Even though you should use it, be aware of where you are in relation to the main system. Also, if the microphone is not wireless, be careful to step over the cord if you're moving to avoid tripping. If you have the option, wireless is usually better. If it's the kind that clips to your clothing, make sure you put it in a spot that works. This is more important than it spoiling the looks of your outfit. If you clamp some microphones to one side or the other, it can be hard for people to hear you when you turn your head even slightly. Always test it to be sure it will work for you the way that you will actually use it.

Don't Go Off to the Races

Have you ever listened to a speaker who is rushing through his information? Sometimes, this is because he's nervous and can hardly wait to sit down again with everyone else. Other times, it is because he has a faster than average rate of speech. There are statis-tics for this, but most people do not measure them-selves, so here's a better gauge. If in your daily life, people listening have trouble staying with you or miss things you've said, you likely talk faster than most people. Regardless of the reason, you do need to make a conscious effort to slow down so that your audience can understand you without becom-ing confused or frustrated. You don't want listeners to have to work at listening to you. Otherwise, as with low volume, what is the point?

My Grandmother is a Southerner who has lived in Tennessee much of her life. Culturally, if you have loved ones in that area, you'll have noticed they tend to speak at a different rate from people who live farther north. When I am talking, she has to actually watch my lips to try to keep up with what I'm saying. I'm speaking too fast for her comfort. When she speaks, I have to hold my breath to stop myself from asking her to hurry it along and sit on my hands to avoid making that rolling motion with my arms or tugging action as though I could pull the words out faster. We have opposite tendencies. What we need to do is adapt to each other better as an audience of one. I need to slow down for her and she needs to speed up a little for me so that we are adapting to each other's needs. Although I've never heard her speak in public, I'm guessing that she would be one of the few folks who really would need to increase her rate of speech.

Most people need to decrease their rate. Much like practicing being louder, you can practice going slower as well. Take it to the other extreme and go at such a slow pace that it feels weird and sounds strange. Again, this will change your comfort zone little by little, so that you will become accustomed to going slower and realize that it is possible. Remember to breathe deeply when you're practicing so that you will remember to take time for that during your actual speech. By the way, this is one of my biggest personal weaknesses! If I don't make a conscious effort, I will go too fast for most of my audiences. It is a constant struggle and I get very excited about my listeners and topics so I have to really make a point of not rushing.

Do Not Fill It Up, Please! (Pausing)

One of the most used filler words or sounds is "um." Other ones you'll often hear include "ahh," "like," or "you know." However, these are not the only ones. Any phrase that is used over and over again to fill space between thoughts is unnecessary. It interrupts the smooth flow and can be quite distracting. Usually when I ask my clients what a smooth speech sounds like to them, they answer that there are little or no fillers, but rather a fluency that makes it easy to listen.

Some people use fillers because they have gotten into the habit of doing so in one-on-one or small group conversations. We will try to keep the floor by making a sound that lets others know that we have not completed our point yet and want to finish what we're saying. We suspect, often due to past experience, that if we are silent while searching for the right way to convey the rest of our thought, some other greedy Gus will jump in and interrupt us.

My sophomore year of college, I was taking an Interpersonal Communication class and we were reading, "That's Not What I Meant," a book on conversational style by Deborah Tannen. It was then that I realized that my roommate, Nicki, and I had very different ideas about pausing in talking to each other. We had been assigned randomly, so we didn't know each other prior to sharing our little dorm room. I had noticed that Nicki didn't always have a lot to say. I had already tried asking her direct questions in conversation so she would know that I was interested in her opinion. It wasn't like she was shy and we clearly liked each other and became friends quickly and easily. But something still seemed strange to me. When I read the part about pausing in Tannen's book, I immediately understood. I had a much shorter sense of pauses in conversation, while Nicki clearly had a longer preference in turn taking. It occurred to me that while I'd been wondering why she sometimes didn't respond, she was probably curious about why I'd ask a question and then start talking again. I made a point from then on to directly ask for her opinion and then count to 100 in my head. Sure enough, if I shut up long enough for her to get a word in edgewise, she always had plenty to say.

Much of the time, you may have to utter an extra sound to keep the floor in conversation, but this is rarely true when you're speaking in public. In our society, public speaking is generally, mostly one directional. Even when a speaker is somewhat interactive, unless she has established a ground rule of inviting the audience to jump in whenever they wish, the listeners usually won't. If audience members do, it's often because they are confused or have a question, which can be a good reason for them to assert themselves into your flow. More often than not, they'll listen unless you ask for their input. So, you don't need to keep the floor, it's yours.

As with the other auditory aspects, you can practice pausing in your speech and practice taking the fillers out of it. When you force yourself to pause and stretch it for longer than what seems comfortable, you recognize that when you pause, you don't faint and the world keeps turning. When you're speaking in front of your audience and you're trying to decide how best to explain something or attempting to remember where you wanted to go next, pausing is OK. And normal. Searching for a word or phrasing that you want to use is spontaneous and sincere and therefore possibly even endearing to your audience. Unless you do it every few sentences, it will be fine and it won't seem that you're disorganized. This is also a factor that rarely goes the other way. I've only heard a couple of speakers throughout my entire career who paused too long, so that you really did have to wonder if they remembered anything more they wanted to say. Most people need to have longer pauses and silent ones.

You can even use pauses for emphasis once you get more accustomed to them. When you've said something profound or cited a startling statistic or different perspective from the norm, give it a chance to sink in for the audience. Pause to allow them to process it. Occasionally, it's worth pausing and then repeating the last sentence or asking them directly to really consider what that means to them.

Speakers who are adept at utilizing pauses effectively almost always sound more confident.

Bueller... Bueller... (Inflections)

Monotonous speakers like the teacher in the movie "Ferris Bueller's Day Off" are tough to listen to for any length of time. When we hear a voice that seems to drone on in the same tone for very long, we get bored, feel sleepy, become restless or even agitated. This makes it difficult to catch all the content and consequently makes it harder to take away value. When you're speaking you need to vary your tone. Using different inflections with higher or lower pitch can make you sound more interesting. You know what's coming right? Practice going very high and very low with your voice to the extent of being silly with it. In theater and broadcasting, actors and anchors do lots of exercises to get their voices warmed up and more open.

In fact, variety is the spice of life when it comes to the sounds of speaking. Although you do need to adopt better habits if you have some disruptive tendencies, you also need to change it up on all these aspects. Vary your volume, rate, pauses and tone for effect. Your voice is one of the tools you can use to be a more dynamic speaker.

You can also use instructions to yourself in your notes to remind you to do whatever you've practiced. It is good to put these in parentheses or a different color or type to distinguish them from your content so that you do not read them out loud to your audience. You might put (SPEAK UP!), (slow... down...), (breathe...). Once you know how it will sound, how will it look?

ACTION ITEMS – Chapter 11:

• Write down at least a couple of habits that you have related to the sounds of your voice that you could improve.

• Practice taking those to the other extreme to broaden your comfort zone in that area. Either practice out loud by yourself, or if possible, videotape yourself, or best of all, practice in front of others and get their feedback on whether or not you've actually changed.

• Jot down reminders to yourself about these habits in the notes you'll use during your real speech.

"Nothing succeeds like the appearance of success."

~ Christopher Lasch, author

Chapter 12 – Out of Sight Visuals

Remember that you have more than one sense. Obviously, an audience hears a speaker's voice. However, you can do a great deal to appeal to your audience's sense of sight as well. Your appearance, eye contact, facial expressions, gestures, movement or use of space and visual aids can all enhance your message, making it richer for your audience to watch while they listen. Stimulating two of their senses will engage them more deeply.

<u>Appearance Matters</u>
How you look and dress will affect the audience's view of you and sometimes of your message as well. Many of us would like to live in a world where appearances do not matter, but the reality is that people are human and do get an impression of us based on how we put ourselves together. Be conscious of what you choose to wear so that it is right for the occasion, timing and setting. And as with everything else, the most important thing is that it is appropriate for the audience. If you're speaking to a suit-wearing crowd, then you should also wear one. If even some people wear suits, then you probably

should. You want to err on the side of dressing the same way as do the most formal people in the audience. If you are speaking at a huge charity dinner event and it's formal or semi-formal, then you should match that level of dress. If you're not sure what is appropriate dress, then ask your gatekeeper who is bringing you in or ask someone who has been to the event in the past how this group defines "formal" or whatever term they've used on the invitations. If, however, you know for certain that the entire audience will be very casually dressed for a speech, then do not wear a suit. While it is acceptable to be slightly more formal than your audience, you don't want to be so different that they won't relate to you as comfortably. Although appropriateness is the chief concern, you do want to try to pick something you'll be comfortable in as well. You don't want to be fiddling with your clothing. If you know that's a habit you have, then avoid scarves or jewelry pieces that move when you move, or anything that you would be inclined to adjust frequently. Mostly, you want something that fits the audience and the occasion and that you also look good in and feel good in for yourself.

The Eyes Have It!
In American society, eye contact is crucial. This aspect will vary for some other cultures. However, here directly looking at your audience will connote confidence, truthfulness, and respect. Speakers who have strong eye contact tend to engage their listen

ers, connect with them better and are trusted more by their audiences. You will hear parents sometimes say that they can tell when their kids are not being truthful with them because they don't quite look their mom or dad in the eye. It is the same theory here. You will have much more credibility that what you're saying is true and worthy if you look directly at your listeners. Some speakers will scan the room, look over the heads of audience members or look to the side often. This will usually hurt your credibility. In a room of 30 or fewer people you can usually look every person in the eye during a few minutes if you make a point of doing so. When you have a larger audience, you do have to do a little more looking at areas of the audience without making quite as direct contact with as many individuals. If you are speaking to a huge audience of more than 1,000 people in a large auditorium with a public address (PA) system, here's what you can do. In your mind, divide the audience into six sections, your front left, front middle and front right, and your back left, back middle and back right. Treat the sections as though you have six listeners and you're making a point to include them all. It is a fairly easy way to include the back of the room especially, and they'll likely connect with you better without even necessarily realizing why.

If you get nervous, some people have suggested you should look at the most friendly or familiar faces so you feel more confident. If you must do this to get going, so be it, but I strongly urge you to try to look directly at as many people as you can when your audience is small enough. Otherwise, you're sort of giving up on the rest of them. If you settle in to speak primarily to the friendly faces or the front row or the middle lane only, you are risking alienating the other faces, the back row or the sides of the audience. People will sense this and not feel as included, again, even if they're not aware of the cause. When you practice, pretend that you have many people in the room by putting out many chairs or imagining that each lamp, table, or piece of furniture is another listener. Try to make direct eye contact with each of the fabricated audience members as you speak. If you are doing a practice run with real listeners, have them spread out as much as possible so that you have to reach them with your eyes.

If you have a tendency to read your notes, then you probably put too much in them. Your speech should never be written out word for word like a script because you will be more likely to read it. Cut out much of the content on your notes. Change sentences to phrases or make phrases shorter, just enough to jog your memory about what you want to talk about next. You should not be looking at your notes and glancing at your audience, but rather glancing at your notes and looking at your audience.

Let's Face It

You've probably heard the saying, "Smile and the world smiles with you." This is certainly true for audiences. The people listening will mirror much of what you do — smiling, frowning, making eye contact, posture, laughing, etc. If you are anxious, the attendees will be as well. If you are comfortable, they will be. If you are having fun, they will as well. You set the tone. Often, this is largely conveyed by your facial expressions. When you relax and smile at the audience, you are showing that you like the group and that increases the chances the group will like you back. Some would say that your goal as a speaker is not to get the audience to like you, and that sometimes you even want to stretch their growth by telling them things that are tough to hear, which means they might not like you. For the most part though, having a mutual interest with your listeners will open their minds to you and therefore to your message, so this will usually be of help to you.

One thing to beware of is frowning. For many of us, our concentrating face is a frown. When we do that, the audience will probably do it back. Sometimes, when you see that the audience is frowning, you may be somewhat uneasy, thinking that the people are angry or really confused. Often they are concentrating or just mirroring your own face! Videotape yourself in advance or give your speech in front of a mirror to see what your face looks like when you are focusing on thinking. Then try to put your facial features back to a neutral setting while saying the lines that made you frown so you can learn to relax those muscles instead of tensing them while discussing that particular subject matter.

Be sure that your facial expressions match your message. In the past, some newscasters were criticized for reading bad news with a smile or happy look on their face. They had been trained to smile for the camera, but delivering something negative is the one time when you should frown, look sympathetic or at least neutral. For your purposes, you should accept that listeners tend to trust your nonverbals (eyes, face and movements) more than your verbals (words) because they are much more subconscious. So, people will assume that your nonverbals are the true message when they contradict what you're saying.

Once I went with Jim, a CEO I worked with, to a television taping for a Teacher of the Year Award. He was supposed to make a brief congratulations message from his company, a couple of sentences to the nominated teachers in that region. He had a fairly serious face. When the speech was played back for us, Jim did not look like he meant what he was saying. His words were positive, but his face was very stoic. I knew that he was truly proud of and happy for the teachers and you could even hear it in his voice, but his face did not match what he was saying. When I explained this to him and asked him to try smiling while delivering the words, I realized that would look like he was trying. Instead, I suggested he really think about what these teachers had done to warrant their nominations so he could focus on the awesome achievements and what they did for their students. This would allow his natural emotion to show. He tried again and it was better, but still not consistent with the level of enthusiasm of the words.

When I told him that, he said, "But is it going to be too much? I mean I want to be professional and not look goofy right?" I responded that I didn't want to offend him, but that there was practically no chance of that. He laughed, did it again and his presentation was natural and smiling. I knew the teachers watching would feel sincerely complimented by his message.

Use Your Space: Gestures, Body Movement, and Stage Presence

Using hand gestures that go along with what you're saying can aid in getting your message across. It also gives your hands and arms something to do that is purposeful, making it less likely you'll be fidgeting. People have asked me if it's OK to put your hands in your pockets. Generally, I would not recommend doing this. It's preferable to use all the tools you have, gesturing and standing up straight with good posture. However, there are some speakers who have such a relaxed manner that keeping their hands in their pockets works for them. If you have a laid back personality, are a confident speaker (you're not hiding your hands or slouching away from the audience), and have a clear passion for the topic, then it is possible you can get away with it. There are speakers who can stand at a lectern, never move, never gesture, never come out from behind it, yet have such an engaging way of speaking, and often a great sense of humor, that they can pull it off successfully. However, these speakers are few and far between for most audiences.

The majority of us need to use our space and eliminate physical barriers like a lectern between our audiences and ourselves. If you have gotten used to standing behind a lectern and don't know how to kick the habit, take small steps, literally. Come just to the side of it so it is not actually between you and the crowd. You can still touch your notes from there. Next time, try coming out to the side and then taking one step away from it, and next two steps before coming back. You might eventually realize you've been away from it for a while and really don't need it at all.

There is a concept called "immediacy" that has to do with the physical closeness of you to others. If you are closer to people, you will connect with them better. This is within reason. We've all experienced the boundary crossing of close talkers, people who sit right next to us in empty movie theaters or stand too close to us when we're waiting in line. Sometimes this behavior is culturally influenced. However, for speakers, it's not likely you're going to be so close you're violating social norms and those audience members who feel that too close sense easily will probably not sit in the front row. Due to this immediacy, you should walk to one side of the audience and talk there for a bit and then do the same with the other side. This makes more of the listeners feel included. However, do not pace. If you go back and forth too quickly, you will seem anxious and, as I've explained before, your audience will get anxious with you. If there is a middle lane, it can be great to walk to or at least toward the back to establish that connection with the people in those seats. Like gestures, walking gives your feet purposeful movement, which cuts down on foot tapping or weight shifting from one foot to the other like you're swaying.

Visual Aids
Should you use them? If they will add to your presentation, then the answer is yes. On the other hand, they're not worth using if they aren't very powerful, aren't big enough for the back of the room to see clearly, or distract from your message instead of enhancing it. Too many speakers use visual aids because they think they're supposed to, but the way they use the aids only detracts from their presentation, making them look less professional.

DO NOT:

• Pass around aids because it's disruptive, and if it's a printed sheet, then the audience will read it instead of looking at you, reducing that important eye contact connection

• Look at your visual aid instead of your audience; just like with notes you should only glance at the aid yet stay connected with the audience

• Use the color yellow in words, graphs or anything that isn't naturally yellow because it is like invisible ink and will not be seen by most of the audience

• Throw things at your audience (like prizes or candy for questions answered) because it is not worth the risk of hitting someone, which I have seen happen

• Use PowerPoint only because you think you must; unless it is such an automatic expectation of that audience culture that it will surely affect your credibility if you skip it

• Have a script or anything close to it or too much text if using PowerPoint because the audience members don't read and listen at the same rate, so they'll switch back and forth between looking at your text and hearing your voice and will quickly be off and missing content

• Read text to the audience because they can read on their own and if there's enough text in a row for you to be tempted, then it's probably too many words already

• Have only words on your PowerPoint because if it is visual, then the whole reason to use it should be to show pictures, graphs, or aesthetics that have more depth than merely text (so do not use more than 20 words per slide)

• Have a copy of the PowerPoint sitting at every spot because they will read it, often end up on a different page from where you are, therefore missing content, and also missing the eye contact connection

• Have a ton of slides in PowerPoint — the general rule should be no more than 10 slides if you can

DO:

• Use visuals if what you're saying cannot be explained as well without seeing an example (such as a landscaper showing before and after pictures or an architect showing photographs of a home he designed)

• Make statistics more meaningful — numbers are exact, yet still can be difficult for us to grasp or really imagine so show a line or bar graph to compare or contrast

Consider this example from an online article at www.4faculty.org describing the different learning styles of adults 18 years and older. Based on a survey from Diablo Valley College in California, most people fall into four main styles: Visual/Verbal (prefer reading), Visual/Nonverbal (prefer images), Auditory (prefer listening), and Tactile/Kinesthetic (prefer touch/doing).

Some do show a mix of styles, which is labeled "Balanced." You will notice that of the 17,624 people included in the statistics that follow, the highest percentage are visual learners. This supports the idea of using visual aspects to enhance your presentations to appeal to the majority of listeners. On top of that, though, see for yourself the difference in the two types of reporting of the findings — first through words only and then represented in a graph.

Words:

While 17% were Tactile/Kinesthetic learners, the next group was the 23% who are Balanced among more than one particular style. The next group was Visual/Verbal (readers) at 30%, then Auditory at 32% of participants. Finally, more than any other style, 43% fell into the Visual/Nonverbal (images).

Graph:

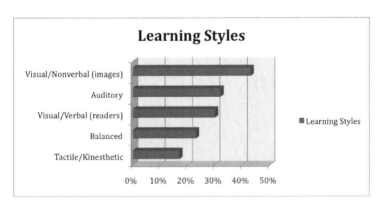

Remember that the reason to use any visuals is to tell a story or enhance one. The story here is that more people are visual learners than any other type and those visual folks would likely find it easier to grasp that concept by seeing the above graph than by reading the paragraph above it. This brings us back to our next "do" item with visuals:

• Use them to tell a story, a trend, or a change

• Practice with the aids so you know how you'll refer to them, get used to them, and how much time they could add to your overall presentation

• Leave handouts at the back of the room if you want the audience to have a take away sheet, rather than putting them on tables or spots

• Include visuals from the audience's world that they will recognize

Once while speaking to the Kansas City Regional Association of Realtors (KCRAR), I used PowerPoint and included the group's own logo and some of the pictures of homes from their KCRAR website so that while making a point about visuals and audience connection, I was modeling an example of what I was teaching them to do. They gave me feedback that my use of the logo was a compliment and they liked seeing the pictures that were familiar to them. They also appreciated the fact that I had taken the time and effort to find and use items they were already proud of and took my PowerPoint images as a gesture of respect from me as their speaker.

ACTION ITEMS – Chapter 12:

• Because you don't see yourself speak in the same way you can hear yourself, you must find out what visual habits you have, if any, that need improvement. Consider feedback you've already received from audiences, videotape yourself, or ask people to watch your practice speech so they can tell you what you could do better. Then, practice those changes.

• Practice direct, inclusive eye contact either with real listeners or, as mentioned earlier, with empty chairs. If you have to move in order to see each face (or chair), then practice doing that.

• Ask yourself what visual aids would really enhance the content of your speech and what would be the best way to display them — PowerPoint, posters, or handouts at the back of the room. Consider what this particular audience expects or prefers.

• Practice using your gestures and your space (with movement instead of only standing still), letting your face respond naturally to your words, and practice with your visual aids if you're using any.

"I never could make a good impromptu speech without several hours to prepare it."

~ Mark Twain

Chapter 13 – Practice Makes Much Better!

Some people always practice before a speech and others almost never do. Some claim that they present better if they don't practice because they feel more natural and less forced. This usually means that when they have practiced, they've written out too much of a script. The reason to practice is that things sound different when you hear them out loud. Sometimes you realize that your main points should be in a different order, the transitions should be clearer to flow from one idea to the next, or you decide to use a better example for support. The best way to practice is to do a dress rehearsal, much like theater performers. This means you should replicate the actual presentation as much as you can. Using the room, the technology, some listeners, a video camera, your notes and your timing will all aid you in tweaking your speech to best fit all aspects of your audience and occasion.

Room for Improvement
If you can practice in the same room where you will speak, that is ideal. Then you get a feel for the lay-

out, acoustics, temperature, and sometimes even distractions such as poor lighting or outside noise that you'll be up against in that spot. If that's not possible, try for a similar size and shape room.

Also, if you will use any microphones, projectors, or equipment, make sure you do a run through to be certain everything is working. You should always plan for technology to fail. Know what you'll do if the microphone doesn't work and have a backup and several extra batteries of the right size. Bring hard copy notes if you're doing a PowerPoint in case the presentation doesn't pull up correctly. If you have a few slides you absolutely need the audience to see to understand your main points, you'll need to have a backup handout of those as well.

Do not tell your audience about the PowerPoint or website or technology that you had planned to use. It doesn't matter if it's your fault or not; it will look like it is. Calling attention to something you can't use or show doesn't do any good. There's no reason for you to look disorganized by depending on technology. Furthermore, saying what's missing from your presentation will imply that the listeners will now be getting something less valuable, putting a negative slant on the speech. You should practice using your PowerPoint and any other visuals so that you get comfortable with them, know how you'll explain them and sense how long they take.

<u>Listener Feedback Is Invaluable</u>

Having coworkers, friends, or family spread out as listeners can be very helpful. They can give you feedback about your strong points, what ideas needed clarification, when your delivery was most natural, and when the flow could have been smoother. There is no substitute for this practicing to an audience. Giving a speech to an empty room is simply not the same.

There is an advantage to already having delivered it to other people that will usually make you less nervous as well. Chances are the first time you give a speech, you'll be nervous, so if you can give it a few times, you'll keep getting more confident. Having others listen to you can also help because they hear things through their own frames of reference so you can learn how some of your wording or examples could be viewed differently from how you intended. It reminds you that your real audience will also bring their own perspective to the table and will likely take things in another way as well. You can't usually anticipate every possible perspective, but a practice audience can enable you to consider some of the common misperceptions that could occur during the actual presentation.

It can be very difficult for audiences to catch all your main points, particularly if you're not the most structured speaker. To avoid this, a good exercise is to ask your practice listeners what they thought the main points were. If you get several answers or people aren't sure how to answer that question at all, then you probably need a clearer preview and you need to clarify which are the key ideas in the body (bulk) of your speech.

Another thing that speakers almost invariably get as feedback from others (be it practice or real) is that they didn't look nervous. This absolutely shocks many people because they were so sure that their voice was cracking or their face was red or their expression was stricken with fear. So ask your practice listeners whether you sounded confident or nervous. They may well tell you how confident you looked. That will surely make you more at ease when you give the real speech.

Lights, Camera, Action!

If you don't have people who can listen to you practice, the next best thing is to videotape your speech and then watch the video. Many people are not a fan of this so they don't do it. However, if you don't have a practice audience, this might be the only way to hear spots where your volume drops off, catch yourself frowning, hear if your fillers are prevalent enough to be distracting or see that you are fidgeting. We are often our own toughest critics, so use this to improve, not to beat up on yourself. Oftentimes, we are pleasantly surprised by the fact that we don't look nearly as nervous as we feel so that can be a boost. Remember, too, as I said earlier, that most audiences don't see your nervousness to nearly the level that you experience it.

Notes and Timing

Be sure to practice using the same notes you'll use for the real speech. The best idea is usually to use note cards so that if your hands shake, you won't make that rattling sheet sound that makes you even more nervous. Also, it is much easier to find your place on a note card, which clearly won't have as much writing on it as a larger sheet of paper. Still, don't cram too much text onto each card, defeating that purpose. Never write out a whole script. You will read it if you have too much in your notes. Also, don't try to memorize your speech word for word. It should be different every time. If you speak from memory and change even one little thing, you can get flustered. Furthermore, you don't leave yourself the flexibility to react to the audience and questions or nonverbal reactions.

Always number your note cards! Use the same spot, such as the top right corner of each card.

Write out more of your introduction than you do the rest of your speech. You're likely to be most nervous during your first 30 seconds in the front of the room. Once you get going, your confidence in-creases as you relax and see that people seem to be interested. Also, be sure to practice enough to be especially comfortable with your introduction for this same reason. You should, though, try to prac-tice all the way through from start to finish a few times. If you practice to a point and stop, particu-larly if you keep stopping in the same place, then you will get used to that and will likely stop at that point in your actual speech. If your speech is 60 minutes or less, you should be able to practice a few times. However, if you are conducting a half day or full day training or other long sessions, then it might not be very realistic to run through the whole presentation several times. In addition, you'll also want to incorporate some interaction or activities to get the audience more involved during a lengthier speech. Still, you can practice the gist, the order and your main points.

It can also be extremely helpful to time yourself. Again, if you have 60 minutes or less, time your presentation exactly. If you know you tend to ramble, ad lib, or somehow use all the time allotted, then give yourself less time. If you've been given an hour, plan for 45 minutes, if given 30 minutes plan for 20 minutes, and if you're in a networking group where you're given 30 seconds, plan for 25 seconds. You'll have plenty of things to stress over, so take this factor out of the equation and be certain that you can stay within the time limit. Even if you've been given hours, you can jot down how much time you want to spend on each main point and each audience activity.

Sometimes people have asked me if it is possible to practice too much. Although most people could benefit from more practice, I do agree that there are some folks who can overdo it. If you practice a few times, put away the presentation for a day or two, then come back to it and practice a few more times, that should be good. Usually, in four to six times of hearing it, separated by some distance from it, you will be able to catch anything that needs to be stronger, clearer, or more relevant. Of course if you have practice listeners, they will have given you feedback from their perspective that you can also incorporate into your final version. Chances are you will make some changes that will enhance the over-all presentation. You'll probably be quite comfort-able with your information and how your audience could perceive it and use it. Past that amount of practice, it does seem that certain types of people either begin scripting or memorizing so that they are saying exactly the same thing each time, losing the natural explanations that are more sincere. Or, some speakers will work themselves into a frenzy, getting more stressed because they are building it up in their mind to be such pressure. Remember that perfection is not the goal, connection is. You need to remember that your presentation is not about you, but about the audience. If you have prac-ticed at least three times (so you know you're not giving yourself an excuse to skip practicing alto-gether) and find you've begun to memorize or stress more versus less with each run through, it is time to put the speech away and visualize the audience us-ing it.

Remember Jeremy with Aflac from the Storytel-ling Chapter? I worked with him and also his two State Training Coordinators, Jen and Ryan, prior to their an-nual State Kick-off Meeting. We were able to have them practice in the actual conference room with some of their technology, timing each person's part with the three of them giving each other feedback in addition to my comments. It was as close to being able to do a dress rehearsal as speakers usually get. After the actual meeting, they got numerous compliments, with many people saying it was their best State Meeting ever. All three speakers indicated that they felt better prepared than ever before and that the practice had forced them to complete their notes, adapt to feedback, and improve their speeches.

The best way to get better at speaking is to practice not just before each speech but also by giving more speeches. Take every opportunity you can to incorporate everything you're learning. Join organizations such as Toastmasters, networking, or education groups where you get chances to speak. The more you speak in front of real audiences, the better you will get at it. Then, you'll be enjoying it more and getting even better still. Success breeds success!

As you speak, practice different ways of interacting with different audiences as well. This is the last aspect of speaking you need to incorporate.

ACTION ITEMS – Chapter 13:

• Do as close to a dress rehearsal as you can — in the room, with the microphone, using the technology, incorporating the visual aids and with the actual notes you will use, timing yourself on each run through of your speech.

• Have people listen, if possible, to give you feedback on everything — main points, stories and support, language, sound habits, visuals, and overall connections and impressions they get from an audience perspective.

• If no people are available, then videotape yourself and examine those same aspects.

• Adapt to either your listeners' feedback or, if using video, to your own impressions to make all those aspects fit as well as possible with your actual audience, not just in your delivery, but in your notes as well.

"We have two ears and one mouth so that we can listen twice as much as we speak."

~ Epictetus, Greek philosopher

Chapter 14 – Time Flies… Interacting with Your Audience

Ironically, speakers who get pretty nervous tend to hang on to the floor (control) very tightly. The thing is when you give the audience some input, you are putting the focus more on them and less on yourself, which most often makes you less nervous, giving you a moment to breathe if nothing else. It also gives the speech more of a conversational feel so that it doesn't seem quite so formal or high pressured. There are many ways to interact with your audience, especially when there are fewer than 100 attendees. There are also strategies that work well, no matter how large the audience. You can ask your listeners questions, give them activities, and field their questions (which can include handling the tough types of audience members before they ruin it for everyone else).

<u>To Be Open or Not to Be Open, That Is the Question</u>
When you have a fairly large audience (more than 70 people) or a short time limit (10 minutes or less), it's best to stick to closed-ended questions. This

means that the question in a normal conversation could be answered with either yes or no. With an audience, rather than have people shout out, it is best to phrase the question to ask for one or the other and look for them to raise their hands in response. For instance, you can ask, "How many of you speak in public on at least a weekly basis?" You can even raise your hand to show that is how you want them to indicate their answer. Even in a huge auditorium, you can glance out and get an idea of the numbers. In a crowd of thousands, it can be one way to see if you are engaging the back rows of the audience. Do not ask more than a few questions here and there though because listeners will get tired of raising their hands, and you'll need to mix it up more than that regardless of the audience size.

Closed-ended questions are good to confirm early on that you were right about some of your educated guesses about your audience, especially if you don't know them well. If you're speaking to accountants and you think that they have a busy season leading up to tax day, but you're not sure whether there are other deadlines during other times of the year, you can ask them how many would say that spring is their most stressful time of year. If you're wrong, and not many answer that way, then you know not to refer to it since you'd be missing the mark. Asking permits you to adapt to actual feedback instead of trying to guess from their nonverbals if they're bored, confused, or just generally concentrating. If you're right, then you can take a little more time on that topic direction since most of them have that seasonal challenge in common with each other.

If you have an audience of fewer than 70 and a time limit of more than 10 minutes, you can use some open-ended questions that can be answered with many different responses. You can even do this in a huge auditorium if you have microphones placed around the room or a few helpers passing them around the room. Just plan to include this question period in your total speech time. This allows listeners to be much more involved in your speech, which usually means they'll relate better and connect more with you, your topic and the rest of the audience. Also, you should be aware that you might have to rein them back in and you must be willing to do so. Some interaction is great, but you don't want a free for all with many people talking at once, which can be frustrating and makes it difficult to follow. You'll need to be an adept facilitator and sometimes you might have to directly regain control. For example, you can ask listeners what the most stressful part of their job is or their favorite part. If many people start speaking at once, you can point to individuals or tell them you'll take two more answers. You can also use a white board (as long as everyone can see it from back of the room) to write their responses on it. This helps keep the focus at the front of the room. If you do that, try your best to write down the actual words they said as a gesture of respect. Don't paraphrase because the point is to get their wording, not your own. If things become too chaotic, you can just say, "Let's get back on track folks." Or, you can tell them you're going to move on from that question.

Also, be prepared for the opposite result from the audience taking over the floor. If you get silence or hear the proverbial crickets chirping, decide in advance how you'll handle this situation. Give them time to answer. If you ask a question, think you have paused, but then start talking before anyone has a chance to respond, the listeners may be insulted, feeling as though you didn't really want their input. You can take a drink of water to force yourself to wait a few moments. You also could ask them to write down some answers to the question first so they've definitely had time to think about it. Sometimes, if you really get no responses, you have to be willing to first give an example of your own to establish trust (remember, it's reciprocal). You share with them so that they'll share with you. Make sure it is a safe question.

My client and colleague, Jeff, is particularly good at interacting with his audiences. However, he ran into a challenge once when he began with an open-ended question, "What are your fears?" Jeff is a very self–aware and open person. He'd be comfortable answering that question in front of a crowd. However, most people don't want to share something as deep as fears with an audience they aren't very close to, so he didn't get many answers from the listeners. He corrected well and gave some examples to establish trust and get the group feeling more comfortable. When Jeff and I discussed his speech later, we changed some of the order of his speech so that he would first have told some examples before asking them about fears. That way, he would have established that safe environment. Also, we reworded it to phrase his question less directly, such as asking what are some common fears that audience members know someone who has? That way, it could be their own, or someone else's fears so that answering didn't require them to be quite as vulnerable. Yet he would still get them involved with an open-ended question.

You need to accept that people often don't want to share private matters with people they don't know well or individuals they want to impress. That's why you shouldn't ask them to volunteer information that they perceive will make them look bad. Also, don't set them up for failure. Don't ask a question, either closed or open, and then after they answer, tell them they're wrong. This can feel like a smack down to the audience. People put themselves out there by either raising their hands or calling out a response and then were punished for taking that risk, which leaves them feeling foolish. This will almost always be a deterrent from further participation, even from members who were not the ones who answered incorrectly before.

Other times, if you really want them to interact with you and you can tell you have a shy or truculent bunch, you might want to joke a little and give them a hard time. Let the people know you appreciate their perspective and would like to hear something from them so that they are leading you in the right direction. Usually, someone will step up to help if you've framed it in a positive light. And you can even allow them to steer a little of the topic direction when you have room for it in your time limit.

Activities

If you have more than an hour, you probably need to give the audience something to do besides just listen. Certainly, if you are conducting any kind of training that is three hours or more, you must include some sort of activity, be it individually or in groups. Human attention spans simply won't last for hours at a time only listening, no matter how dynamic the speaker is. Use your creativity to make the activity something this particular audience will enjoy doing. If there is an added advantage to them working together, such as team camaraderie, then it's probably best to break them into groups. When doing so, if you've had any problem people who tend to chat with their neighbor or shoot each other negative looks, this is a good time to split up those pairs. Ask people to form smaller groups; five people is usually an ideal number. Count people off and tell them to take their belongings and move to their new spot. You may have to include four or six people per group, depending on the size of your audience. More than six won't work well because you start to get a group within the group and three is a whole animal on its own because of people's tendency to pair off, leaving a couple-plus-one dynamic that is rarely ideal.

Have a purpose in mind for each activity. You want people to have fun but also learn something. Explain instructions clearly so they know what they're doing. Give them a goal or two to accomplish and give them a time limit. Be pretty specific. If the audience is made up of designers, maybe you have them build something together (task oriented). If the audience consists of management, you can have them discuss industry trends (idea generation). It could be 10 minutes for something that's fairly light for team building or 30 minutes for a more complex subject such as strategic planning prioritizing. With some audiences and topics, it can be fun to create some friendly competition among the groups. Just be aware that regardless of the age of the attendees, everyone will expect there to be a winner and probably want a prize, even if it's something small.

With auditorium seating where it's not easy to group together in chairs or at tables, you can do individual activities. Or, there may be reasons even in small groups to have each person work independently. If you're discussing goal setting or career planning, it may be preferable not to work as a group. You'll still need to give clear directions and set a time deadline. You can also ask attendees to complete further steps when they leave your speech or training; if you do this, provide a deadline for that as well. This tactic can be a powerful way to lead people to act on the tools and training you've given them, reinforcing the value they take away with them.

Whether one at a time or together, after the activity, you should explain precisely the point of the exercise if you didn't do so beforehand. People need to know why the exercise was a valuable use of their time, even if it seems obvious to you.

Fielding Questions

When the audience members ask you questions, remember that this usually shows at least some degree of interest, so you should be flattered, not flustered. Even queries that seem tough can be viewed as an opportunity to clarify ideas, contradict misconceptions or win over skeptics. As soon as you hear certain questions, you realize that other people are also likely to be wondering about the same thing. If that is the case or if the answer is very brief, go ahead and give it. If you aren't sure whether or not this is a question that many listeners would have, then ask how many others want to know that. If one-third or more of the group raises hands, it's probably best to go ahead and address the answer fairly thoroughly to the room at large. If just a handful are curious, you should give a concise answer and move on quickly. If only one or a few people are interested, or you don't want to answer in front of everyone because the answer is relevant to only one individual, then say it depends and you'd be happy to talk with that person individually at the end or set up an appointment for another day so you honor the group's time now. You might also have to do this at times when one listener just doesn't quite seem to get it but you sense from others' feedback that the rest of the audience already does.

You should not spend an extended period of time helping one person at the expense of the entire group — public speaking is not individual coaching. Sometimes, one person railroads the show with his own personality quirk. Here are some common ones and tips for handling them diplomatically.

The Show Off: This is the audience member who wants to be the speaker or at least to let everyone else listening know that he knows all or better or at least more than most. This person might interrupt, answer every question, or correct others.

Tip: Although this person seems to have a huge ego, often the opposite is true, and what he is showing is his insecurity about being smart enough or good enough. So, let him be right if he is. Compliment him briefly, but don't elaborate or make a big deal of it. You want to acknowledge this information but not reinforce the behavior. Sometimes, you'll have to joke about not making that person do all the work or that as much as he has to contribute, you want to spread the opportunity around and hear from everyone. If you have to get direct with him, then keep it friendly. Thank him for his contributions and let the others in the group know it's their responsibility to answer the rest.

The Cynic: This person will be negative. She will put a dark spin on content, motives and especially results. She lets you know that it doesn't matter what you do, things will still go wrong and turn out poorly. She expects the worst from people and situations. She may not be vocal but she might still scoff or roll her eyes. You will sense her disdain.

Tip: This can also stem from a type of insecurity. If you expect everything to go badly, then you will experience less disappointment, guarding against really caring so that you don't get let down or embarrassed for putting yourself out there with something. (I confess to doing this at times as a National Football League fan!) There may be nothing you can say to shake this one person out of her funk during one speech. You can try asking what would happen if things did go well to get her to visualize it and articulate. You could tell her that her energy and attitude can actually affect the outcome, but she might still not believe you or be willing to take the risk. What you need to do is, if you can't get that one person to come around, let her know that for the sake of the larger group, you're going to ask everyone to be positive at least out loud so that no one is putting a damper on the spirits of others.

The Challenger: This person likes to argue. He probably does so in one-to-one conversations as well. For everything you say, he thinks the opposite and might even share examples of why you are wrong and he's right. He may get downright belligerent or could stay pretty matter of fact.

Tip: Especially if he stays matter of fact, this is probably just his style and not a personal attack on you, even if it feels like it is. If he gets emotional, there could be a topic history or context that also has nothing to do with you. So, either way, do not take it personally and do not rise to his level of emotion. The best way to diffuse an emotional reaction is to stay calm yourself. He can't escalate as far without your engaging him. However, if you sense it is more personality and the content actually brings up interesting points, then take the opportunity to refute the other side of the items but do so with evidence, logic, and examples, not with emotion or your own "expertise" (I win the argument because I'm the speaker).

These are some of your worst-case audience members taken to the extreme level. Usually when you have a difficult person, his behavior will be much less pronounced than these scenarios but you can still handle it in a similar way. Fortunately, these situations don't happen very often, especially in all adult, volunteer audiences. If people are required to attend an event, you might get a challenge here or there, but even then, establishing the value to them early on and setting a friendly, professional tone at the start will usually be enough to keep people from acting unreasonably. Remember that most audience members want you to succeed and are looking forward to hearing how you can help them. Again, questions most often indicate interest, which is a good thing.

ACTION ITEMS – Chapter 14:

• Write at least three questions (open or closed, depending on your audience size and time limit) for your audience in your actual notes.

• Anticipate what their answers might be so you know how you could incorporate those and move on to your next points, but don't assume that you know exactly what they will say.

• Imagine what questions or concerns they might have for you and either address them directly or know how you will handle them if they do arise.

• Leave time for your questions, interactions, activities (allow more for these) and their questions when practicing and timing yourself.

"High achievement always takes place in the framework of high expectation."

~ Charles F. Kettering, inventor

Chapter 15 – Great Expectations

We've taken a good deal of time in this book to consider what the audience expects. We have discussed analyzing who they are, what is important to them, what they are looking for from you, the topic, and the occasion. We have described examples of people using this other-oriented approach, not only in public speaking, but also in all communication. If you approach every interaction thinking about other people's perspectives, the chances increase dramatically that you and the others will have a mutually satisfying outcome.

When you spend time organizing information for your audience, choosing words that they will relate to and stories they'll remember, you are involving them in your process before you ever step in front of them. That process is what you can and should repeat with every speech, instead of repeating the information and words so that your speech ends up being the same, regardless of who is listening. Remember that this does not mean that you are simply telling the listeners what they want to hear. You need to first connect with them so that you can then challenge them and even push them past their comfort zones to try something different so they can achieve even more exciting results.

You can and should set expectations of your audience. You can do it at the start, through your actively worded main points, with inspiring stories at the end, or all of these. Your call to action in your closing line especially can tell the audience what you expect them to do with the information you've imparted. This will reinforce the value you have provided, and that makes them more likely to repeat what you've said, sharing that value with others, essentially spreading the word about your message. They will understand your points even better when they explain them to others. They are also even more likely to act on what you've told them when they become passionate enough to repeat it. When this occurs, you will have created spokespeople for your ideas. It's not that hard. It's not that time consuming. It's not nearly as nerve-racking when it's not about you. It merely takes a willingness to step out of the focus while stepping into the spotlight.

So, what I expect of you the reader, is to go and do this! Make it about your audience in every speech, in every meeting and in every relationship. You have the power to change the lives of others, which will in turn change your own.

This is why Leaders Speak.

ACTION ITEMS – Chapter 15:

- Take every opportunity to speak when you can.

- Remember that it is not about you.

- Utilize the audience perspective every step of the way.

- Lead.

- Speak.

LIST EXAMPLES

Lists 1–5 and Resulting Main Points

Tip: Do Lists #1, #2, and #3 before you start organizing content ideas, when possible do them before narrowing your purpose and sometimes before even choosing a topic if that has been left to you.

List #1 – Yourself

Client: Lisa, Founder & Chairwoman of Board for Safe Place for Kids

* = Top 3 Most Defining – If you could only use 3 words, what would they be?

Compassionate
Friendly
* Energetic
Organized
Confident
Thorough
* Passionate
Supportive
Innovative
* Appreciative

List #2 – Your Audience – going to a 2nd and then 3rd level of depth

Client: Lisa, Safe Place for Kids

Audience: Northland Chamber of Commerce

◯ = Also on List #1 – Yourself

If we know these:	We also know these:	And also know these:
Level#1	Level #2	Level #3
- Involved	- Care	- (Compassionate)
- Busy	- Limited time	- Stressed
- Political	- Agendas	- Accomplished
- Tight knit	- Know others	- Loyal
- (Passionate)	- (Energetic)	- (Confident)
- Community	- Protective	- Like a family
- (Supportive)	- Giving	- Generous
- (Organized)	- Structured	- (Thorough)
- Growth	- Ambitious	- Promoting
- Leaders	- Responsible	- High standards

List #3 – Your Common Ground

Client: Lisa, Safe Place for Kids

Audience: Northland Chamber of Commerce

From 1st level	From 2nd	From 3rd
- Passionate	- Energetic	- Compassionate
- Supportive		- Confident
- Organized		- Thorough

Tip: Have Lists #2 and #3 handy before you start the next lists. After you've created List #4 and put a star by your own top priorities, stop before you do the circles. Then reread Lists #2 and #3 so that you have your audience's perspective fresh in your mind and are coming at your topic and list of content items from their point of view. Also, you will be reminding yourself what you have in common with them, which can help you ultimately choose main points that work best for both you as the speaker and the listeners in your audience.

List #4 – Your Priorities

Client: Lisa, Founder & Chairwoman of Board for Safe Place for Kids

Audience: Northland Chamber of Commerce

* = Top Three Most Important to the Speaker

◯ = Top Three Most Important to the Audience

- *Safe housing
- *For children
- *Build structures
- Kids in state custody, abused or neglected
- NOT run program
- NOT Habitat, but we're like it for kids
- Partner with organizations
- Orgs like Juvenile County, Counsel Center
- Program vs. corporation
- Give to community
- The building
- Give grant money
- Not "Safe Place" (at YMCA or QuikTrip)

List #5 – Audience Priorities

Client: Lisa, Safe Place for Kids

Audience: Northland Chamber of Commerce

⬭   - Transfer circled words from List #4 as Important to the Audience

- For children
- Give to the community
- Give grant money

ADD to Audience list:
- Kids in the same area as Chamber who are homeless
- Kids have to be sent to another city because not enough facilities here

RESULTING MAIN POINTS
(with active verbs to start wording) that both speaker and audience will relate to best and consider important:

1. Help children (from both speaker and audience priority list)
2. Build buildings (from speaker priority list)
3. Give money (from audience priority list)

ACKNOWLEDGMENTS

This book would not exist without the help of so many people that it is difficult to thank them in only a few pages. God has changed me, merely in the writing of it, placing on my heart the memories of so many blessings that I can't count them all. However, I will at least hit the highlights.

My husband, Adam, suggested over three years ago that I write this book. He's the more natural writer in the family, so I took that as a great compliment. He encouraged me, committed to help me edit it, pushed me (but not too much), helped me with writing decisions and editing, and supported me in every way possible. He has come up with innovative ideas and directions for my business, helped me implement them, and provided bigger vision for the future of my company. In spite of my resistance, he has challenged me to open my mind about changing my company name, brand identity, website, social media and basically invited me to join the current age and technology for the sake of the book and the business. His faith in me has been amazingly inspiring, and I have found that I can do more than I thought I could because he believes in me. God has given me a gift in Adam to help me be a better version of myself. I have felt an indescribable joy in sharing this journey with Adam as we have found yet another wonderful aspect of our already fulfilling partnership. I can't imagine having done any of this without him.

One of my oldest and dearest friends happens to be an extremely talented graphic designer. Stacy Adair created my book cover, letterhead and most of my new brand identity (including logo, color scheme and elements for the website, business cards, and offer pages in this book). She put a tremendous amount of time and energy into all these pieces, making everything sharp and consistent. She has given me incredible support during these projects and completely changed my business in a way I could not have done myself.

Another of my closest friends, Jill Pace, does marketing and public relations, so she has been a huge help in editing copy for my website, video, offer pages in the book and media pitches. In addition to all that, she poured her time and effort into being one of the first readers of my book and gave me excellent suggestions and perspectives as a marketer, PR expert, corporate leader, teacher and public speaker that made it much stronger.

My sister-in-law, Katie McFarlane, is not only one of my best friends, she has been one of my biggest supporters for my entire career. She was the first person, besides my husband, to read and dig through my entire book looking to improve it, which meant there were a lot of changes to be made. She provided me with so much poignant feedback that I must say that it would not have been the same book without her involvement. After adapting to her comments, I felt immediately more confident that this book could really help people and for that I am eternally grateful.

Others who donated their time to reading my book and giving me their opinions were my wonderful brother-in-law Neil McFarlane, and generous friends Jon Lile, Rena Striegel and Jonathan Whistman, all of whose views I value highly. Also, Jonathan helped me by sharing a great deal of wisdom and advice as my business coach, including keeping me accountable when I was first writing the book.

My parents, Phil and Dianne Bumpus, and my in-laws, Jim and Lissa Cross, have made it possible for me to run a business and write a book because they really do provide a village to help raise our children. They've spent their time, energy and much effort to this end and to keep us close as a family. I simply couldn't have accomplished this without their support and the kind of unconditional love that makes me willing to dream big and go after it.

After my husband Adam suggested I write the book, three other people separately told me this as well. Two were Scott Horstmann and Kathleen Andersen, both clients who allowed me to use parts of their stories in the book and both of whom I now call friends. The other was Dr. Ivan Misner who also graciously provided the Foreword for the book. I've learned that when three people I trust tell me the same thing, that's God nudging me to get moving, so I listened!

The number of people who have encouraged me on this path really is too large to count. In addition to those already named, my biggest cheerleaders in the process of writing this have been my very dear friends Danielle Brady, Amy Petersen, Amy Pleimling, Jenner Van Horn, Kam Heskin, Jeff Miner, my entire BNI chapter, my Lunch Bunch ladies and my awesome brother-in-law Stephen Cross.

My college adviser, Hank Tkachuk, led me to discover and start down the road of teaching and training that is my absolute passion, for which I can never thank him enough. My more recent advisers have helped me know what to do with the book through Steve and Bill Harrison's Quantum Leap program, especially coaches Geoffrey Berwind (storytelling) and Mary Giuseffi (image). Also, I appreciate my editor Debby Englander, particularly for helping me use a more active voice in my writing, and Martha Collins for doing the final proofreading.

My young sons Jason and Isaac are the most amazing creatures God ever put on this earth. They support me, even though they're young and that touches my heart so deeply, I could burst with love for them. They are growing into such little gentlemen that it makes me think that maybe I'm getting better at teaching them as I learn from others around me.

Finally, all the clients who have trusted me with their own business roles are the book. They are the examples that caused me to know this process for public speaking works. Seeing them experience change in their careers and their lives was what became too worthwhile not to write down to share with others. There would be no book without the people whose stories you read in it.

Thank you Jesus.

I'VE READ THE BOOK SO WHAT IS NEXT?

You can start standing out from other speakers right NOW!

At readers' requests, Jody is offering two FREE tools to get you started. These tools will help you begin using the strategies from this book before every presentation.

VISIT WWW.LEADERSSPEAK.COM, ENTER "AUDIENCE" AS THE CODE (IN THE BOOK SECTION) TO RECEIVE THESE FREE TOOLS

AUDIENCE ANALYSIS-ONE GROUP

ARE YOU SPEAKING TO LISTENERS WHO ARE ALL FROM THE SAME ORGANIZATION?

When audience members are all from one company or from different companies but all united through one membership organization, there are aspects you can easily identify that the listeners have in common with each other.

AUDIENCE ANALYSIS-MULTI GROUP

ARE YOU SPEAKING TO LISTENERS WHO ARE ALL FROM DIFFERENT ORGANIZATIONS?

When audience members are all from different companies AND are not united through one particular membership organization, it can be more difficult. You need to draw some likely conclusions about what type of audience member might be attracted to your topic, event or the marketing for your speech. Imagine what listeners would probably have in common with each other.

LEADERS speak

WANT TO BRING LEADERS SPEAK TO YOUR CITY?

DO YOU WANT TO BE A LEADER IN YOUR FIELD?

INCREASE YOUR CLIENTS AND REVENUE?

CREATE SPOKESPEOPLE FOR YOUR BUSINESS IN EVERY PRESENTATION?

YOU CAN DO ALL THIS WITH OUR LEADERS SPEAK PROGRAM!

Our participants will learn to harness the power of speech to create growth, expansion, and demand from their potential client base during our **Leaders Speak group coaching program**. Get individualized, professional advice from a public speaking expert, while enjoying an interactive, dynamic, and supportive small group atmosphere.

PART 1 - YOU REALLY ARE A MIND READER - Learn to prepare in a way that leaves the audience feeling you were speaking directly to them.

PART 2 - EVERYONE LOVES A GOOD STORY - Learn to turn dry facts, figures and information into a story your audiences will relate to, remember & repeat.

PART 3 - PRACTICE IN PRIVATE, LOOK GREAT IN PUBLIC - Learn to smoothly deliver your message to your audiences and receive group feedback to enhance your presentations.

Leaders Speak isn't just a book! It's a program that has changed many careers and lives by transforming people's public speaking. Will yours be next?

FOR MORE INFORMATION PLEASE GO VISIT WWW.LEADERSSPEAK.COM

Made in the USA
Columbia, SC
08 September 2019